T0065244

Transformation, Transition, *and* Tranquility

Thomas J. Horne B.S. M.Div. Th.D.

TRANSFORMATION, TRANSITION, AND TRANQUILITY

Scripture quotations marked KJV are from the Holy Bible, King James Version (Authorized Version). First published in 1611. Quoted from the KJV Classic Reference Bible, Copyright © 1983 by The Zondervan Corporation.

iUniverse books may be ordered through booksellers or by contacting:

iUniverse
1663 Liberty Drive
Bloomington, IN 47403
www.iuniverse.com
844-349-9409

ISBN: 978-1-6632-1602-1 (sc)
ISBN: 978-1-6632-2872-7 (hc)
ISBN: 978-1-6632-1603-8 (e)

Library of Congress Control Number: 2021918022

Print information available on the last page.

iUniverse rev. date: 09/08/2021

Contents

Introduction ix

Part I: Transformation

Chapter 1   Preaching the Word 1
- Why Preach the Word? (The Foolishness of Preaching) 1
- The Importance of the Spoken Word 3
- Conformed 3
- Why Transformation? 5

Chapter 2   A Renewed Mind 7
- A Renewed Mind 7
- Remembering Jesus 9
- Remember So You Can Pass It On 12
- Why Remember? 12
- In the Absence of Jesus 13
- Giving Thanks 14
- Releasing of Beneficial Blessing 15
- Giving Thanks is an Act of Faith 15
- Giving Thanks Sends a Message 16
- The Greek Word and Definition of Giving Thanks 16
- Giving Thanks Is an Offering of Praise 16
- Count It All Joy 17

Part II: Transition

Chapter 3   What is Transition? 23
- Why Transition? 24

Chapter 4   How to Transition 27
- Why Transition Isn't Easy 28
- Pressing 29

- Knowing Who You Are 31
- A Blessed Man 33
- How Are We Blessed? 33
- Calling It Like It Is 35
- I Will Bless the Lord 35

Chapter 5   Blind Bartimaeus's Transition 38
- Waiting for a Transition 39
- The Waiting! 39
- Initial Transition 40
- Transition Takes Time 41
- The End of Time 43
- The Accuser of Our Brethren 45
- Why Accuse the Brethren? 45

Chapter 6   Evolving in Transition (Spiritual Evolution) 47
- Salvation (The beginning of Spiritual Evolution) 47
- Evolving in Obedience 48
- Why Is Obedience Important? 49
- Obedience unto Death 52
- Obedience Earns God's Respect and Trust 53

Chapter 7   Evolving in Transition (Evolving through Suffering) 56

Chapter 8   Evolving from Feelings and Emotions 61
- How to Deal with Feelings 63
- The Most Important Part about Dealing with Feelings 64
- Encouraging Yourself 66

Part III: Tranquility (Peace, Quiet, Rest)

Chapter 9   What is Tranquility (Peace, Quiet, Rest) 71
- What is Tranquility? 71
- How Do We Obtain Tranquility? 73

Chapter 10 Why Tranquility? (Peace, Quiet, Rest) 77
- Perfect Peace 77
- How Do We Keep Our Minds? 78
- Hold Fast the Profession (Confession) of Faith 79
- Trusting God 80
- Faith versus Trust 81

Chapter 11 Eternal Tranquility? (Peace, Quiet, Rest) 84

Chapter 12 Final: Transformation, Transition and Tranquility 87
- Caught Up Together 87

References 91

Introduction

While living in a changing world as believers and facing changing times, it's important that after we transform to new creatures in Christ, we continue the transformation as we transition to a higher level of ministry. Transformation is not just a spiritual thing we undergo; it is a mental and physical undertaking as well. We should transform in the way we think, transform in the things we do, transform in the places we go, transform in our attitudes, and transform in the habits we practice.

Transformation doesn't happen overnight. The apostle Paul said, "I'm trying to apprehend that which I'm apprehended of Christ Jesus" (Philippians 3:12).

Paul was stating that he was not there yet—and neither are we. We have to keep transforming and transitioning every day until we reach a place of tranquility. Tranquility is having a harmonious relationship with God that is accomplished through the Gospel and having a sense of rest and contentment. This doesn't mean resting *from* work; it means resting *in* work. This means that you can continue the work, but you should have a sense of peace and rest while working.

"Thou wilt keep him in *perfect peace,* whose mind is stayed on thee: because he trusteth in thee" (Isaiah 26:3). The vine's complete expository dictionary defines the Greek word *teleios,* which is translated to the English word *perfect,* meaning wholistic, well-rounded, or complete peace. When we reach a place of tranquility, we obtain perfect peace (wholistic, well-rounded, or complete peace). The purpose of this book is to help every believer reach his or her fullest potential of a higher calling while transforming, transitioning, and finally reaching tranquility.

PART I

Transformation

Chapter 1

Preaching the Word

> Preach the word; be instant in season, out of season; reprove, rebuke,
> exhort with all long-suffering and doctrine. For the time will come
> when they will not endure sound doctrine, but after their own lusts shall
> they heap to themselves teachers, having itching ears; And they shall
> turn away their ears from the truth, and shall be turned unto fables.
> —2 Timothy 4:2–4

I will try to keep this simple. First of all, "preach the word" in this scriptural verse means preach the Word of God. "In the beginning was the word, and the Word was with God, and the Word was God" (John 1:1). This verse did not tell us to preach *a* word; it told us to preach *the* Word.

A word can be anything. The Greek word "Logos" means "anything written; a saying or statement." An "exit" sign is a Logos. A "stop sign" is a Logos. A "bathroom sign" for men or for women is a Logos. A Logos can be "anything written; a saying or statement," but the Word in the Bible is not *a* word. It is *the* Word of God.

The Greek word for the "spoken Word of God" is "Rhema," which also means "the preached Word of God by the Holy Spirit."

Why Preach the Word? (The Foolishness of Preaching)

> For after that in the wisdom of God the world by
> wisdom knew not God, it pleased god by the foolishness
> of preaching to save them that believe.
> —1 Corinthians 1:21

For years, I questioned why God called preaching foolishness. One day, God boldly told me why. He said, "I called preaching foolishness because I had to call a man to tell another man how to live right." I have not looked at preaching the same way since God told me that. God plainly explained it to me. He said, "If one man can hear and obey me, then any other man should be able to also." It is foolishness to tell another man what he can hear from God himself, but this is the foolishness that God has called us preacher too.

I want to be the first to say that I am not a fan of theatrics or attention-getting gestures in the pulpit. I really feel that the pulpit should be a holy and sacred place where God chooses Sunday after Sunday to speak and manifest Himself through His preached Word. We are living in a day and time when the world is competing with the Word of God. It is trying to steal the attention of sinners and the attention of God's people. I can somewhat understand why the foolishness of preaching pleases God.

Preaching has two sides; one side is the sacred and holy side, which carries the anointed preached Word with signs and wonders from God, and the other side is the foolish things we do as preachers to get the attention of the people. I actually think it's weird and somewhat foolish to set a bush on fire just to get a man's attention, but that is what God chose to do to get Moses's attention.

After God got Moses's attention, God spoke to him. The devil is using the world to steal the attention of the people. God uses the power of his preached Word to compel people to come to Him (Romans 1:16), but that's just part of it. Sometimes people need to see a burning bush.

John Wesley, one of the most quoted and noted theologians of the eighteenth century, was asked why his revivals were attended more than all the others. Wesley said, "I set myself on fire, and people come to watch me burn." The other side of preaching is the foolishness, which is the things preachers do to get people's attention. This is the foolishness of preaching that pleases God.

The Word of God "is the power of God unto salvation to all that believe" (Romans 1:16). The preached Word of God is the power of God; this is the "*dunamis*" (the Greek word for power) of God when preached or spoken (rhema). The preached Word of God is God's power, which is compelling humans to change their ways of life. The foolishness of preaching is also used by God to "to save them that believe" (1 Corinthians 21).

The Importance of the Spoken Word

"And upholding all things by the Word of His power" (Hebrews 1:3). This verse lets us know that *all* things are supported and controlled by the power of God's Word.

"We ought to give the more earnest heed to the things which we have heard, lest at any time we should let them slip" (Hebrews 2:1). This verse tells us that if we, as believers, don't take the Word of God seriously and give the Word of God "more earnest heed to the things which we have heard" by meditating as David did day and night, we can "let them slip."

> For if the word spoken by angels was steadfast, and every
> transgression and disobedience received a just recompense
> of reward; How shall we escape, if we neglect so great
> salvation; which at the first began to be spoken by the
> Lord, and was confirmed unto us by them that heard him.
> (Hebrews 2:2–3)

This verse explains how we can escape punishment for neglecting to hear and obey the preached Word of God, which was first spoken to us by Jesus and then spoken to us by those of us who were called to preach the Word. There is "recompense of reward" (punishment) for those who "neglect so great salvation."

Conformed

> And be not conformed to this world: but be ye
> transformed by the renewing of your mind.
> —Romans 12:2

According to Vine's Complete Expository Dictionary (VCED), the Greek word for *conform* is *summorphizo,* which means "to make of like form with another person or thing, to render like."

The apostle Paul states, "I beseech you therefore, brethren" (Romans 12:1). The word "beseech" in Greek is *parakaleo,* which means "to call to one's side: to call to one's aid" (VCED). Paul was saying that he was calling aid with the mercies of God. He was calling for God's mercy to assist and aid us while we "present your bodies a living sacrifice, holy, acceptable unto God" (Romans 12:1).

Paul knew he would need God's help in presenting his body as a living sacrifice because of the flesh. "For I know that in me (that is, in my flesh) dwelleth no good thing" (Romans 7:18). It's not easy to present something—the flesh—to God that keeps warring against you.

> But I see another law in my members (flesh), warring
> against the law of my mind, and bringing me into captivity
> to the law or sin which is in my members (flesh).
> (Romans 7:23)

The flesh wars against the spirit because the flesh does not want to be brought under subjection to the Word of God and be presented as a living sacrifice, holy and acceptable unto God. The desire of the flesh is to stay conformed to this world and not go through the transformation, but this is something we have to do—with God's grace and mercy. Paul said, "I call to your aid or to your side" with the mercy of God, and His grace will help you accomplish this.

The Greek word for conform is *summorphizo,* which means "to make of like form with another person or thing, to render like." The flesh has a desire "to make of like" the world or to have us adopt ways of the world. If we are not strong enough to fight worldly trends, we will become like the world. It is important to stay under the Word of God in order to defeat the ways of the world.

The other portion of that definition of summorphizo is actually becoming like another person or thing or "to render like."

> Be not conformed to this world: but be ye transformed by
> the renewing of your mind. (Romans 12:2)

We are advised in this scripture not to be conformed to this world and to be transformed by the renewing of our mind. Transformation can only take place through the Word of God. The body can not conform, be brought under subjection, or be presented as a living sacrifice until your mind is renewed through the Word of God.

After becoming born-again believers, it's imperative that we begin to renew our minds with the Word of God. An unrenewed mind will always present problems in the flesh. Being born again does not automatically renew your mind. This is something we have to do by studying God's Word.

> But I keep under my body, and bring it into subjection (to
> the Word): lest that by any means, when I have preached
> to others, I myself should be a castaway.
> (1 Corinthians 9:27)

The flesh will always crave the things of the world, but a renewed mind in the Word of God will be able to bring the body (flesh) under control or subjection to the Word. This is called transformation:

> And be ye transformed by the renewing of your mind.
> (Romans 12:2)

Transformation continues to take place after being born again through a continuously renewed mind every day.

> In thy word do I meditate day and night until I become
> a tree. (Psalm 1)

We have to stay in God's Word—day and night—until we become strong enough to control our bodies and present them as a living sacrifice unto God.

Why Transformation?

The world is changing every day, and every generation is getting more intelligent and more divisive. The enemy is using a changing world to attack the kingdom of God with laws, political movements, and subliminal brainwashing via social media. Social media and economic pressures affect jobs, finances, homes, and families.

We need individual transformation and every person examining themselves as the scriptures state. We also need to know what we need to cope and survive in a changing society. We must transform and then transition. As people of God, it wasn't meant for us to always stay the same throughout this Christian walk. God wants us to become better so we can go further and do more. Becoming better is transformation, and going further and doing more is transition.

Finally, it is our inheritance and privilege to improve and be better. God wants us to achieve higher heights and greater callings to ministry. According to Ephesians, God wants us to obtain a more powerful anointing with all the spiritual blessings in heavenly places. God wants us to prosper and be in good health. He wants our souls to prosper!

Chapter 2

A Renewed Mind

And be not conformed to this world: but be ye
transformed by the renewing of your mind.
—Romans 12:2

A Renewed Mind

The Greek word for "transform," according to the *Vine's Complete Expository Dictionary,* is *metamorphoo.* According to Google, a *metamorphosis* is "the process of transformation from an immature form to an adult form in two or more distinct stages. It's a change of the form or nature of a thing or person into completely different one, by natural or supernatural means."

The Greek word *metamorphoo* means "to change into another form, and to undergo a complete change." This definition implies that the spirit, soul, and body have to undergo a complete change. After undergoing the transformation of salvation, we must undergo a complete change of mind. The mind has to be renewed and undergo spiritual changes and social changes. Proverbs 23:7 states, "For as he thinketh in his heart, so is he."

We have to change the way we think. Instead of saying, "I think I can," just say what the Word of God's says: "I can do all things through Christ which strengthens me."

Secondly, we have to stay away from negative people. People with negative mindsets will cause you to become negative. When you change your mindset, you can then change your behavior. Behaviorism is birthed from a mindset: "for as he thinketh in his heart, so is he." If you think you are a failure, you will begin to speak failure and behave as a failure; behaviorism is birthed from a negative mindset.

Philippians 2:5 states, "Let this mind be in you that was also in Christ Jesus." Paul was saying that the mind of Christ is available to us; all we have to do is "let it be in us" by studying the Word of God.

The mind of Christ does not come to us just by asking God or praying to God. We have to study the Word of God, fellowship with people of God in his Word, and meditate on the Word of God.

> Study to shew thyself approved unto God, a workman that needeth not to be ashamed, rightly dividing the word of truth. (2 Timothy 2:15)

We have to find quality time to study God's Word and meditate in it. The mind of Christ develops in us as we study and meditate on God's Word. As believers in Christ, we must have the mind of Christ. This is not just because of the probability of the flesh taking over; it is because of the danger not having the mind of Christ might put us in by.

> For to be carnally minded is death, but to be spiritually mined is life and peace. (Romans 8:6)

We put our lives in danger by having a carnal (worldly) mind. We might even face death. To obtain peace and tranquility, which is in the last section of this book, we need to have the mind of Christ or a spiritual mind.

> Thy shall keep them in perfect peace whose mind is stayed on thee. (Isaiah 26:3)

According to *Vine's Complete Expository Dictionary, perfect* means "complete, lacking nothing; a well-rounded life." If you keep your mind focused on the Word of God, God promises to keep your life complete, well managed, and lacking nothing. When we seek the things of the kingdom first, as Matthew's Gospel states, everything else will automatically be added by God as He promised. According to this scripture, we have to keep our minds focused on His Word.

> For the weapons of our warfare are not carnal, but mighty through God to the pulling down of strongholds. Casting down imaginations, and every high thing that exalteth

itself against the knowledge of God, and bringing into
captivity every thought to the obedience of Christ.
(2 Corinthians 10:4–5)

Paul explains how to protect your mind. The Word of God is your
spiritual weapon, and it is able to cast down and replace every negative and
worldly thought and even the imaginations of the mind. Using the Word
of God as your weapon will "pull down strongholds" in your mind and in
your life. Anything and everything that the enemy is using to keep you in
bondage when you begin to study and abide in the Word of God will pull
down strongholds and set you free.

After pulling down the strongholds and imaginations through the
Word of God, we have to replace those vacant and blank places in our
minds with the Word of God.

> Finally, brethren, whatsoever things are true, whatsoever
> things are honest, just, pure, lovely, are of a good report,
> if there be any virtue, if there be any praise think on these
> things. (Philippians 4:8–9)

We have to replace the vacant places in our minds with honest, just,
pure, lovely, and good things. Avoid gossip and hearsay. Meditating on the
Word of God is a virtuous thing.

Remembering Jesus

> For I have received of the Lord that which also I delivered unto you,
>   That the Lord Jesus the same night in which he was betrayed took
> bread: And when he had given thanks, he brake it, and said, "Take, eat:
>   this is my body, which is broken for you: this do in remembrance of
> me." After the same manner also he took the cup, when he had supped,
>   saying, "This cup is the New Testament in my blood: this do ye, as
> oft as ye drink it, in remembrance of me. For as often as ye eat this
> bread, and drink this cup, ye do shew the Lord's death till he come."
>   —1 Corinthians 11:23–26

One of the most important things about this Christian walk is that we retain what we *know* about Jesus—and not what we *believe*. It is what we know about Jesus that guarantees us victory and success.

One of my previous books, *The Truth about Faith*, explained how the highest level of faith is knowing:

> If the Word of God says you already have it, you would not have to believe for it any longer; at this point you just Know you have it, and call it into manifestation. You have to walk and live by faith before you can come to the place of knowing. When you Know something is true, you no longer have to believe that the same something is true.

I asked a young lady in my church, "Do you *believe* your name is Jane—or do you *know* your name is Jane?"

She replied, "I *know* my name is Jane."

I told her that as long as she *knows* her name is Jane, she does not have to *believe* her name is Jane. The Word of God is the same way. There are scriptures in God's Word that imply that you can know certain things regarding the Word. This does not mean you are no longer required to believe; instead, it means you can go beyond believing to knowing.

Knowing something from the Word of God can only be stated by the Word of God. When the Bible says "knowing," it means you can actually *know* this as a fact. Knowing something gives you more confidence that it is so because you know it is. Knowing something does not negate the fact that we have to continue to walk in faith and believe in God's Word. It merely presents us with a higher level of faith, which is knowing.

Knowing is a higher level of faith because it is still the Word of God. The Word is faith. Everything about God is faith—even though we know that God is real. It is what you know about Jesus that guarantees victory and success.

Here are a few scriptures in the Word of God that include the word *knowing*:

> *Knowing* this, that the trying of your faith worketh patience. (James 1:3)

And not only so, but we glory in tribulation also: *knowing* that tribulation worketh patience. (Romans 5:3–5)

Knowing this, that our old man is crucified with him, that the body of sin might be destroyed, the henceforth we should not serve sin. (Romans 6:6)

Knowing that Christ being raised from the dead dieth no more; death hath no more dominion over him. (Romans 6:9)

Knowing that whatsoever good thing any man doth, the same shall he receive of the Lord. Whether he be bond or free. (Ephesians 6:8)

And we *know* that all things work together for good to them that love God, to them who are the called according to his purpose. (Romans 8:28)

Knowing that of the Lord ye shall receive the reward of the inheritance: for ye serve the Lord Christ. (Colossians 3:24)

The world will challenge what you know with distractions and temptations. Remembering what we know about Jesus grants us the opportunity to recap the wisdom and knowledge that strengthen and build our Christian walk.

The word *remember* in Greek is *mimnesko,* which means "to call to mind or to remind oneself." We have to remind ourselves every day of who we are and what we can do in Christ Jesus so that the devil can know that we have not forgotten.

The devil wants us to remember bad things and bad times. He wants to keep us down emotionally. Philippians 3:13 tells us to "forget those things which are behind." To move forward, we must forget some things and put them behind us.

On the other hand, remembering a good moment or a good person brings back the essence of that moment and the essence of that person. It is important to recapture that essence of that person and that moment.

When our emotions are low or we are struggling emotionally, remembering a good time, a good person, or a good moment can help us survive.

An old picture, an old song, or an old place can hold fond memories. The memory can hold the essence of a moment and bring back the strength, energy, and excitement of that particular time, which can help us survive our emotional lows.

A good moment is meant to last. It is hard to capture that exact moment again, but if we remember how it felt or what was said, we can carry the essence of that moment with us forever.

Remember So You Can Pass It On

This is my body which is given for you: this do in remembrance of me.
—Luke 22:19

Jesus is saying, "This is My moment, and I am giving it to you. As often as you do this, I want you to do this same thing in remembrance of me. Do this act of communion to commemorate this moment. If you remember this moment, you will remember Me and everything I stood for."

I have received of the Lord that which also I delivered unto you. (1 Corinthians 11:23).

Paul is saying, "I delivered to you the very essence of that moment and the very presence of His body by way of communion. I bring this moment and His presence to you because I choose to remember Him and take Him with me everywhere I go."

Why Remember?

We need to remember before we can be reminded.

But the comforter, which is the Holy Ghost ... He shall teach you all things, and bring all things to your remembrance, whatsoever I have said unto you. (John 14:26)

By letting this mind be in us, which was also in Christ Jesus (Philippians 2:5), and by meditating on the Word of God—day and night (Psalm 1:2)—and we call to remembrance, by the Holy Spirit, that which was originally obtained by studying to shew ourselves approved unto God (2 Timothy 2:15). You cannot be reminded by the Holy Spirit of that which you have not retained, and you cannot retain that which you have not studied to obtain. The Holy Spirit is there to teach and bring back to our remembrance everything that we retain. In the end, we need to remember so we can be reminded by the Holy Spirit.

We need to remember because Jesus said so. Jesus said, "Do this in remembrance of me." We need to remember Him because He told us to do it. For everything Jesus has done for us, Jesus deserves us remembering Him.

When Jesus said, "Do this in remembrance of me," it wasn't for His sake; it was for our sake. Jesus knew remembering Him would make it hard for us to forget Him, what His Word said, and what He did for us. Remembering all of this is what makes us who we are in Christ, and it causes us to be victorious in all things.

In the Absence of Jesus

The absence of a person can encourage a memory of that person. The more you miss someone, the more you remember them, especially in the darkest hours when things seem to be going badly.

> The first day of the week after the Crucifixion, they brought spices to the tomb and found the stone rolled away. And when they entered in they found no body. The men were much perplexed as they beheld two men standing by in shining garments. And the men, as they bowed down their face to the ground were told by the men in shinning garments, "Why seek ye the living among the dead?" He is not here, but is risen: Remember how he spake unto you when he was yet in Galilee, Saying, "The Son of man must be delivered into the hands of sinful men, and be crucified, and the third day rise again. And they remembered his words." (Luke 24:1–8)

Remembering Him will make it hard to forget what He has said to you and what He has done for you.

Giving Thanks

> In everything give thanks: for this is the will of
> God in Christ Jesus concerning you.
> —1 Thessalonians 5:18

First Thessalonians 5:12–22 include instructions for holy living. All of God's Word is His will, but there are some scriptures that point out specifically the will of God. "In everything give thanks" (1 Thessalonians 5:18). It is not saying *for* everything; it is saying *in* everything.

Thanking God for everything indicates that, whether good or bad, we should thank God for it. I don't agree with that. I would rather thank God only for the good. I can't believe that God is responsible for the bad things; therefore, I can't thank Him for things He is not credited or responsible for.

Thanking Him for everything means thanking Him for heart attacks and strokes and other bad things that He did not cause.

> The theft come not, but for to steal, kill, and to destroy.
> (John 10:10)

To me, thanking God for bad things is calling Him a thief. "In everything give thanks" indicates that no matter what you're going through or facing, in the midst of your storm of troubles, give God thanks for the victory, give Him thanks for deliverance, and give Him thanks for overcoming every bad thing you encounter.

The second part of that verse states, "For this is the will of God in Christ Jesus concerning you." What is the will of God concerning us? "Giving thanks in everything" is the will of God, and it concerns us. It's not for trees, birds, fish, cats, dogs, or any other creatures; it is for humanity! Humans are the only creature created to glorify and give thanks to God because we were created in God's image and after His likeness. This is why giving thanks is so concerning to us. We were created to give Him thanks and worship Him.

Verse 12 to verse 22 is all spiritual instructions for Holy living, but verse 18 is the only verse that indicates that this particular verse and instruction specifically is God's will concerning us. Giving thanks is more important than all the other verses because there is something in giving thanks that the other instructions don't have: "divine spiritual benefits."

Releasing of Beneficial Blessing

One the quickest ways to get another blessing is thank Him for the one you just got. Everybody can count at least one blessing that they have received: food to eat, clothes to wear, health and strength, and family and friends. We have to thank God for the small things, and this will put us in position for bigger blessings. If we can't thank God for the little things, we will find it very difficult to obtain bigger blessings. Giving Him thanks releases blessings and the spiritual power that is needed for our everyday walk and life as Christians.

The next beneficial blessing is thanking God in bad times and bad situations. Thanking God in bad times and situations challenges our focus and changes our focus. There is always something good to be found in every bad situation; we just have to find it and focus on that good thing. When we do this, it will change our whole outlook of the situation. The Word of God tells us to "look not at the things that are seen," especially when they are bad. Don't focus on them, "for they are temporal," which means they are temporary. The Word goes on to say, "but the things that are not seen," which is the Word of God, "are eternal."

Giving Thanks is an Act of Faith

Giving thanks is an act of faith that says no matter what I'm going through, it's working together for my good.

> For I reckon that the sufferings of this present time are
> not worthy to be compared with the glory which shall be
> revealed in us. (Romans 8:18)

The glory that shall be revealed in us is the spiritual blessing that benefits our life and ministry.

Giving Thanks Sends a Message

Giving thanks sends a message to the devil. It says, "In spite of all you tried to do to me, I'm still standing." Giving thanks sends a message to God. It says, "No matter how things look, I still trust You to honor Your Word.

The Greek Word and Definition of Giving Thanks

The Greek word for "giving thanks" is *eucharisteo*, which means "expressing joy in a thankful way" or "expressing thankfulness in a joyful way."

When we find ourselves in a situation and circumstance that dictates hurt, pain, obstacles, and challenges, we try to find the quickest way through or out of it. There is no clear-cut solution other than having faith in God's Word.

This definition suggests that thanksgiving is the expression of joy toward God, and it is therefore fruit of the Spirit (Galatians 5:22). Believers are encouraged to abound in joy. Even if you're not glad or happy, giving thanks is an expression that says, "Even after all I have gone through, I still have joy."

Giving Thanks Is an Offering of Praise

By him therefore let us offer the sacrifice of praise to God
continually, that is, the fruit of our lips giving thanks to his name.
—Hebrews 13:15

Expressing joy by giving thanks when we don't feel like it makes it a sacrificial praise offering. There are times when we feel as though we can't afford to give God a praise offering, but we should give it anyway. This makes it a sacrificial praise offering.

Count It All Joy

> My brethren, count it all joy when ye fall into divers temptations; Knowing this, that the trying of your faith worketh patience. But let patience have her perfect work, that ye may be perfect and entire, wanting nothing. (James 1:2–4)

The first thing I noticed while reading this scripture is that James stated that the "brethren," which means fellow Christians and believers in Christ, should "count it all joy when ye fall into divers temptations." He did not say, "Count it all joy when ye walk into divers temptations" or "Count it all joy when ye encounter temptations." James could have very well meant that, but he said, "Count it all joy when ye fall into divers temptations."

Falling is something that most people don't plan on doing. Although inviting temptation is something that most of us has done, falling into temptation sounds unintentional. None of us likes to fall into anything. The "falling into temptation" James is talking about here sounds unintentional.

The best of us—no matter who we are, how prayed up we are, or how strong we think we are—will someday fall or make a mistake. We will find ourselves under pressure at some point and saying things or doing things that are not right with God. Even though we are born again of the spirit, we are still human and live in this body of flesh. Even at the trying of our faith by temptation, we don't always stand; we all have failed at some point or another.

> For I know that in me (that is in my flesh,) dwelleth no good thing: for to will is present with me, but how to perform that which is good I find not. (Romans 7:18)

17

This verse is no excuse to sin or to allow sin to have its way. It merely states that sin dwelleth in all flesh—not just in the Apostle Paul's flesh. He wrote three-quarters of the New Testament.

In James 1:2, he states, "Count it all joy when ye fall into divers temptations." James is not suggesting that we rejoice or be happy about a failure, a mistake of the flesh, or a failure to withstand temptation. Instead of being angry, sad, or overly hurt by guilt, we should just "count it all joy."

Count it all joy because things could be worse than they are. Count it all joy because God is a forgiving God.

> If we confess our sins, He is faithful and just to forgive us
> our sins, and cleanse us from all unrighteousness.
> (1 John 1:9)

Count it all joy that a "just man falleth seven times, and riseth up again: but the wicked shall fall into mischief" (Proverbs 24:16). Count it all joy that God is a God of second chances. Count it all joy that He is a God of restoration and healing. We should count all these statements as statements of joy when we fall in divers temptations. Count it as a moment of reflection on God's goodness.

James is saying that in counting it all joy, let your trials, temptations, and failures count for something. The Greek word for *joy* is *oninemi*, which means "to profit or benefit from." This means finding something profitable or beneficial out of being tried or failing. While we are going through whatever we are going through, we can start by counting it all joy. Rejoice while reflecting on the Word of God instead of dwelling on temptation or failure. Always remember it could have been worse. Just praise God and "count it all joy" that you have a chance to make things right.

Don't let what you're going through be in vain. Let what you're going through work together for your good. Let what you're going through build patience. Let what you're going through build hope that makes you not feel ashamed. Let what you're going through build boldness and strength. Tell yourself, "I went through this—or I'm going through this now—but I'm going to get something out of this trial so I won't fall next time."

Joy is an action word; it means one needs to show exuberance and emotions in a physical way. Let us change our expressions to gladness.

Adapt a positive attitude and behavior. Sing and clap our hands. Start praising the Lord—no matter how bad we feel or how bad it looks. Nehemiah 8:10 states, "That the joy of the Lord is our strength." When you count it all joy or rejoice, it strengthens your faith and propels you to victory.

Psalm 8:2 and Matthew 21:16 state, "Thou hast ordained strength" and "Thou hast perfected praise." God has ordained strength or has purpose us to be strengthened because of the joy and praise we are expressing. Psalm 8:2 says, "That thou mightiest still the enemy and the avenger." When we begin to joyfully praise the Lord, whatever the devil is doing to us stops.

There will always be times when we will be faced with trying moments—and we won't always pass the test. As long as we are in the flesh, we will make mistakes. We will experience hurtful moments, but getting back up when we fall determines our moving forward.

There is a greater purpose in everything. We have to say, "My purpose is not to keep falling or remaining down because of these temptations. I must get up and keep on going. We must realize what the devil meant for bad is working out for my good.

When we count it all joy, it's sends a message to the devil that says, "No weapon formed against me shall prosper." We have to tell ourselves and the enemy that we are better than where we are, that this is not where I am supposed to be, and that this is not where I want to be. Then say to yourself, "I've got to get up and make this transition."

PART II
Transition

Chapter 3

What is Transition?

But we all, with open face beholding as in a glass the glory of the
Lord, are changed into the same image from glory to glory.
—2 Corinthians 3:18

The Greek word for transition is *Metatithemi,* which means "to transfer or
move to another place." This word also means "a change or passing from
one condition, place, thing, activity, or topic to another."

Once we initialize a transformation, it continues even throughout our
transition. We never stop transforming or transitioning. The apostle Paul
stated, "But we all, with open face beholding as in a glass the glory of the
Lord, are changed into the same image from glory to glory, even as by the
spirit of the Lord" (2 Corinthians 3:18).

We all should seek to do better and be better in this Christian walk,
and this is called *transition*. We are changed into the same image of Jesus
Christ—from one step of His glory to another. This is called transition.

Transition is transferring or moving from one place to another. As
Christians, it wasn't meant for us to stay in the same place in Christ Jesus.
We are supposed to move to higher heights and deeper depths in Him. To
do this, we must make transitions in our Christian walk. Transitioning is
never easy, but it starts with focusing on where you want to go and how
you are going to get there. The best way to start transitioning is to seek
the will of God for your life and pray for direction. This includes abiding
in the Word of God—day and night—as David stated in Psalm 1: "In thy
word do I meditate day and night."

> Not as though I had already attained, either were already
> perfect, but I follow after if that I may apprehend that for
> which also am apprehended of Christ Jesus.
> (Philippians 3:12)

Paul is saying, "I'm not there yet." Paul is continuing his transition. Transitioning never ends. Paul is saying, "I am not already perfect," which is to say I am not yet complete. Paul is also saying, "I am trying to get better by trying to apprehend that for which also I am apprehended of, which is Christ Jesus." This is accomplished by continuously looking into the looking glass of the Word of God, which reflects the glory of God through Jesus Christ and the very image of Him and who we should become.

Colossians 3:3 states, "For ye are dead, and your life is hid with Christ in God." Anything that is hidden need to be found or discovered. Our new life in Christ is hidden until we become mature enough to accept it. We must discover our purpose, which is our hidden life in Christ.

> For precept must be upon precept, precept upon precept;
> line upon line, line upon line; here a little, and there a
> little. (Isaiah 28:10)

God teaches us His Word by the Holy Spirit. It never comes all at once; it is a path of transition.

> Though our outward man perish, yet the inward man is
> renewed day by day. (2 Corinthians 4:16–18)

Our outward man is transforming and getting older every day, and the inward man is supposed to be transitioning and becoming more like Jesus. Transformation and transition never stop until we leave this world.

Why Transition?

Paul states in Philippians 3:14, "I press toward the mark for the prize of the high calling of God in Christ Jesus." A "higher calling" has three main steps: awareness, proactiveness, and persistence.

Awareness is "the ability to directly know and perceive, to feel, or to be conscious of events, objects, thoughts, emotions, or sensory patterns." In this level of consciousness, sense data can be confirmed by an observer without necessarily implying understanding. In the spiritual forum, this means hearing from God, recognizing your situation, and moving by faith.

In order to be aware of our situation and be ready to do something about it, we must hear from God through His Word and the guidance of the Holy Spirit. Secondly, we all should recognize a need to transition to a better place in life. We must recognize that where we are is not benefiting us and that we have been here too long. It's time to move! Finally, we have to recognize how to get where we need to be by studying the Word of God and listening to the Holy Spirit.

Proactiveness states that "(of a person, policy, or action) creating or controlling a situation by causing something to happen rather than responding to it after it has happened." In other words, being proactive is doing something in advance to change the outcome of something that is going to happen or has been happening. Doing something different than what you've been doing. Don't religiously keep doing the same old wrong things and getting the same results. We must head in a different direction with our goals and purpose.

Next, we need to have a total change of mind. A renewed mindset can change your focus and grant a new vision, new ideas, and a new perspective on life. Try to do something that you have never done before—something that will challenge you—and always be open to the guidance of the Holy Spirit.

Persistence is "continuing firmly or obstinately in a course of action in spite of difficulty or opposition." In other words, keep doing the right thing and the things that inspire you and make you happy in spite of difficulty and opposition. Keep doing things that improve you; this is what blesses you, motivates you, encourages you, and makes you better. Have a daily habit of reading scriptures. Find songs to sing and inspiring people to fellowship with. Keep a good daily routine and never give up or lose faith in what you're doing.

I truly believe that there is something better for us to look forward to, to reach, to obtain, and to accomplish as Christian believers. There has to be more to this Christian walk than what we are experiencing or what we've been privy to (going to church, singing, paying tithes/offering, Bible study, Sunday school, and all other Christian activities of worship). These are normal Christian requirements. There has to be a higher purpose for us! We haven't reached it or obtained it yet, and we should press for it.

Transitioning is our inherent right. It is God's will that we improve and be better. "Pressing toward the mark of the high calling" (Philippians 3:14) is all about going higher in the Lord and being better. God wants us to obtain a greater anointing with all spiritual blessings. The Greek word for *pressing* is *Dioko*, which means "to pursue something." We have to know what we're pursuing. "If by any means I must (not I *might*), but I must attain it" (Philippians 3:11). Paul is saying, "I'll do just what I have to do in order to get where I need to be."

We need to tell ourselves that we'll do just what we need to do in order reach that place in Christ because we're not there yet. We have to forget the past and let go and forget about some people in our lives. We have to put away some old habits and pick up some new habits that will benefit us on this spiritual walk. We have to press toward the mark for the prize because it is our inheritance that we are pressing for. It's your time to obtain; this is your season.

Pressing sends a message to people watching us and believing in us. It lets them know that if you can do it, they can too. Pressing sends a message to God that you are not going to give up and that you are still walking by faith and pursuing your goals. Finally, it sends a message to the devil that he can't hold you back any longer from your blessings because you're more than a conqueror. No weapon formed against you shall prosper.

God wants us to "prosper and be in good health, even as our souls prosper." This is called transition.

Chapter 4

How to Transition

Why Transition Isn't Easy

Denise Burns, a writer for Kenneth Hagan's *Word of Faith*, explains why transitioning is not easy:

> Every season is beautiful in its own time. When we're in a season, we're doing our thing and loving it. But when that season starts coming to an end, we begin feeling uncomfortable. We feel like we should go in a different direction. But maybe we're not sure what to do or where to go. In between where we are and where we're going is a gap of time called Transition.
>
> Transitioning from one season to another can be difficult for some people. But we need to realize that the way we leave one season is often time the way we begin the next season. So we want to make a good Transition.
>
> Some people make good Transitions and some don't. Many times people start to gripe and complain. And sometimes they do things that hurt others. When Transitions aren't made correctly, a lot of damage can be done. I don't believe that God wants us to handle a change of season this way.
>
> Transitions don't have to end badly. We don't have to burn bridges every time we move into a new phase in our lives. We can make better Transitions by recognizing when a season is coming to an end. And the way we do this is by listening to the Holy Spirit.

Why Transition Isn't Easy

> When the spirit of truth comes, He will guide you into
> all truth. He will not speak on his own but will tell you
> what He has heard. He will tell you about the future.
> (John 16:13)

Because of fear, transition can be very difficult. The Word of God states that "fear has torment." Change frightens a lot of people because of having to adjust to a different mindset and a different social place (new friends, a new behaviors). A different spiritual place in Christ can be very scary!

Transition may include different physical goals for your body, like losing weight or changing your eating habits. It may include changing how you handle your finances, your marriage, or your educational future. As a parent, transition may include differences in parenting your children or how you entertain new friends. We also must consider mental changes. Having the mind of Christ makes the changes easier because the Holy Spirit will help us in our infirmities and weaknesses.

Making changes to what kind of leader we want to be and how we serve God differently is very important. These can be frightening changes, and they are not easily decided or obtained. However, they can be accomplished with the help of God.

We have to make these sacrifices in order to have a successful transition in our lives. The way we transition is important. Isaiah 28:10 states, "For precept must be upon precept, precept upon precept; line upon line, line upon line; here a little, and there a little:" Transitions should be done a little at a time.

It is the little things we can do to initiate a transition. We can examine our thinking to see if we are thinking the right things. We can ask someone we trust to tell us the truth about what we are thinking. We can pray and seek the Holy Spirit about everything we do or decide. Communicating with spiritually minded people regarding the Word of God can be very helpful.

When it comes to your physical well-being, cut back on foods that are harmful to your health. Only eat them in moderation. Make a decision to eat healthy foods more often. Pick your friends wisely. Choose people who share your spiritual, emotional, and mental values. As a parent, listen to your children more and talk less. As a wife or husband, always find time for each other.

Ask yourself, "What can I do to make me better?" Ask your spouse the same question. My personal transition started with doing a small thing like cleaning up my junky room; just doing that made me feel better about myself.

Transitions don't have to be scary. A little at a time can go a long way toward helping you in your transitional changes.

Pressing

That I may know him, and the power of his resurrection, and the
fellowship of his sufferings, being made conformable unto his death; If
by any means I might attain unto the resurrection of the dead. Not as
though I had already attained, either were already perfect: but I follow
after, if that I may apprehend that for which also I am apprehended
of Christ Jesus. Brethren, I count not myself to have apprehended:
but this one thing I do, forgetting those things which are behind,
and reaching forth unto those things which are before, I press toward
the mark for the prize of the high calling of God in Christ Jesus.
—Philippians 3:10–14

Everything in this Christian walk is predicated on "knowing Him." Learn who Jesus is. Knowing Him unlocks the mysteries of who He really is and who we are in Him. It's who He is and who we are in Him that defines us as believers.

The apostle Paul discovered who he really was when he finally got to know Jesus. Paul explains everything he had gained in life:

I counted loss for Christ. Just for the Excellency of the
knowledge of Christ Jesus my Lord. For whom I have
suffered the loss of all things; and do count them but
as dung, that I may win Christ (the knowledge) and be
found in Him not having mine own righteousness, and

the power of His resurrection; and the fellowship of His
sufferings. (Philippians 3:7–9)

Paul is stating here in these next scriptures that there are things he
needed to do in order to "attain" unto this goal. Verse 12 states, "not as
though I have already attained" either were already perfect (none of us are
perfect) but Paul said "I follow after" which means I am chasing after Jesus;
and will do what I have to do to get more and more of Him. Paul goes on
to say, "but this one thing I do, forgetting those things which are behind,
and reaching forth unto those things which are before, I press toward the
mark for the prize of the high calling of God in Christ Jesus."

Let me break down this scripture. The Greek word for *forgetting* is
Lanthane, which means "to escape notice, to be willfully ignorant of the
things that are before us." We have to willfully escape the things that bring
notice to us of the past. We also have to be willing to block them out and
ignore them because they are there to bring us down. They hold us back,
and they hold us captive to our past hurts and pains. We cannot move
forward if we keep focusing on the past hurts and mistakes. We have to be
willing to forget them and block them out by meditating on the Word of
God. There are some things that we will never totally block out or forget.
This is our "thorn in the flesh."

The Greek word for *reaching* is *Katan Tao*, which means "to come to
a place; to reach, attain to; to stretch forward." We must reach forth and
come to a place of attainment of the things that are before us. The things
that are before us belong to us; they are our inheritance. We should be
tired of standing still and living in the past. There is something better for
us, but we have to reach for them, and we have to stretch out and attain
them. We must, as this definition states, "come to a place" of realization
in life and settle for nothing less.

Finally, the Greek word for *pressing* is *dioko*, which means "to pursue,"
"a footrace," or "to speed on earnestly." Pressing is not easy. When the
enemy puts opposition in our way, this becomes "a footrace." Pressing
means "to pursue" something. We have to know what we are pursuing.

The apostle Paul, in verse 11, states, "If by any means I must: not I
might, but I must attain it." In other words, I'll do just what I have to do
in order to get where I am going, a place that is my destiny. We have to tell

ourselves that we have to do whatever we need to do because we are not there yet. We have to forget about the past and even forget some people. We put down some things that aren't good for us and pick up some better things. This includes better people in our lives and better habits. We must press on because we are pressing on for our inheritance. Our time is now, and this is our season to obtain.

Pressing sends a message to people who are watching us and believing in us that if we can do it then they can too. Pressing sends a message to God that we are not going to give up and that we are still walking by faith and holding on. Pressing sends a message to the devil that our blessings can no longer be held back. Now I know that I am more than a conqueror, and no weapon formed against me shall prosper because if God is for me, who can stop me or be against me?

Knowing Who You Are

In 1 Corinthians 15:10, Paul states, "But by the grace of God I am what I am." One of life's greatest tragedies is not remembering or knowing who we are. Having a solid spiritual and Christian identity is very important for transitioning. It's hard to transition when we don't know who we are. Not knowing who we are puts us in a state of identity crisis. An identity crisis gives the enemy the upper hand in and against our lives. Hosea 4:6 states, "My people are destroyed for lack of knowledge:"

By stating, "By the grace of God I am *what* I am," Paul is saying, "I am more than just a personality (a who). I am what I am." That is the gift part of you that God has created and given to be developed for His glory. We have to see ourselves as more than just personalities:

> But we have this treasure in earthen vessels, that the
> Excellency of the power may be of God, and not of us
> (2 Corinthians 4:7)

In order to avoid an identity crisis, we need to know who we are and who Jesus is. Whoever Jesus is is also who we are in Him. Colossians 3:3 states, "For ye are dead, and your life is hid with Christ in God." Paul, in

Galatians 2:20, says, "I am crucified with Christ, nevertheless I live, yet not I but Christ lives within me,"

We die in Christ, but because of His resurrection, we are also alive in Him. We are with Him. Since our life is "hid with Christ in God," as Colossians states, we need to discover our true born-again identities in Christ.

Galatians 3:29 states, "If ye belong to Christ, then are ye Abraham's seed; and heirs according to the promise." Because we are Abraham's seed in Christ, the promise also belongs to us. Galatians 3:9 says, "So then they which be of faith are blessed with faithful Abraham." This is our true identity. We are what and who we are, as Paul stated, by grace. All we have to do is make the transition to what and who we are through the Word of faith. Be *what* and *who* the Word says you are.

Ephesians is also a discovery of our true identity in Christ Jesus. Ephesians 1:3 states that we are "blessed with all spiritual blessings in heavenly places in Christ." Verse 4 states that we are "chosen before the foundation of the world to be holy and without blame before Him in love." Verse 5 states that we are "predestined unto the adoption to be His child by Jesus Christ." Verse 7 states that we are "redeemed through His blood and have forgiveness of sin."

Verse 8 states that "He has abound toward us in all wisdom and prudence." Verse 13 states that we have "been sealed until the day of redemption with the Holy Spirit." Verse 20 states that "we are seated with Christ in heavenly places." Verse 21 states that "we are seated with Christ far above all principality and power, might and dominions and every name that is named, in this world and in the one to come." Verse 22 states that "He has put all things under His feet and His body which is the church."

Ephesians 2:1 states, "When we were dead in trespasses and sins, that He quickened us and made us alive." Verse 5 states that we were "quickened together with Christ and by grace are we saved." Verse 6 states that "He raised us up together and made us sit together in heavenly places in Christ Jesus." Verse 8 states that "so by grace are we saved through faith." Verse 10 states that "we are His workmanship, created in Christ Jesus unto good works, which God hath before ordained that we should walk in them."

All of Ephesians, especially chapters 1 and 2, helps us further discover our true identities in Christ Jesus.

A Blessed Man

Blessed is the man that walketh not in the counsel of the ungodly,
nor standeth in the way of sinners, nor sitteth in the seat of the
scornful. But his delight is in the law of the Lord; and in his law
doth he meditate day and night. And he shall be like a tree planted
by the rivers of water, that bringeth forth his fruit in his season.
—Psalm 1:1–3

When we become complacent and forget that we are blessed, we have to remind ourselves of what the Word of God says about us being blessed.

First of all, being blessed is a privilege. Second, just knowing that you are blessed empowers you. You have to know that you are blessed before you can be empowered by being blessed. The devil don't want you to know that you are blessed. He wants to keep you ignorant of the fact that you are blessed—so you won't be empowered. Knowing you are blessed is empowering.

The Greek word for *blessed* is *Eulogeo*, which means "to speak well of," "to invoke blessings upon a person," or "to bestow blessings upon what God said."

The first part of this definition, "to speak well of," means a blessed man should be well spoken of and speak well of others. The next part of this definition, "to invoke blessings upon a person," means to "command" a blessing or cause a blessing to come on someone by speaking it on them. The last part of this definition, "to bestow blessings upon what God said," means to bless with the spoken or written Word of God so that the Word of God will do just what it was sent to do. This means speaking blessings on people, situations, and everything that needs to be blessed.

How Are We Blessed?

And the scripture, foreseeing that God would justify the heathen
through faith, preached before the Gospel unto Abraham,
saying, "In thee shall all nations be blessed. So then they
which be of faith are blessed with faithful Abraham."
—Galatians 3:8–9

If we are born again with the faith of Abraham through Christ Jesus, we are "blessed with Abraham." This means that whatever way Abraham was blessed, we are blessed in that same way. We are not blessed because of Abraham; we are blessed *with* Abraham because of Jesus.

> Christ hath redeemed us from the curse of the law, being made a curse for us: for it is written, Cursed is every one that hangeth on a tree: That the blessing of Abraham might come on the Gentiles through Jesus Christ; that we might receive the promise of the Spirit through faith. (Galatians 3:13–14)

> Now to Abraham and his seed were the promises made. He saith not, And to seeds, as of many, but as of one, And to thy seed, which is Christ. (Galatians 3:16)

The blessings of Abraham were promised to Abraham's seed, which is Jesus, but Jesus forfeited the blessing of Abraham so everyone would believe on him and be saved.

> And if ye be Christ's, (if you belong to Christ), then are ye Abraham's seed, and heirs according to the promise. (Galatians 3:29)

We are blessed with the same blessings that Abraham is blessed with through Christ Jesus, which is the seed of Abraham.

Being blessed is more than a state of being. Being blessed is more than an inherited blessed way of life. Being blessed is a mindset. We have to have a blessed mindset. A mindset should be in line with the Word of God and state, "As a man thinketh in his heart, so is he." We should have a positive mindset because we are blessed, but we should believe it in our hearts and know it according to the Word of God. We should think it, believe it, know it, and speak it. Speak the Word of God, which says you are blessed.

Calling It Like It Is

We have to speak blessings on ourselves and on others. If we are blessed, as the scriptures have stated, then we have the same authority as Abraham and Jesus to speak to the mountains of situations and problems that plague our lives daily. We can either bless them or curse them.

> As it is written, I have made thee a father of many nations, before him whom he believed, even God, who quickeneth the dead, and calleth those things which be not as though they were. (Romans 4:17)

> For verily I say unto you, That whosoever shall say unto this mountain, Be thou removed, and be thou cast into the sea; and shall not doubt in his heart, but shall believe that those things which he saith shall come to pass; he shall have whatsoever he saith. (Mark 11:23)

We have to speak to ourselves first and then to the mountains about the problems and situations that arise in our life. Hebrews 10:23 states, "Hold fast your confession of faith without wavering, for He (God) is faithful that promise." In other words, we have to keep speaking and saying what we want until it manifests or appears. We have to keep calling it like it is.

I Will Bless the Lord

The last part of the definition of *blessed* is "to bestow blessings upon what God said," which means to bless the spoken or written Word of God so that the Word of God will do just what it was sent to do. "To bestow blessings upon what God has said" means to bestow a blessing on God himself—because God is His spoken Word—and when we bestow a blessing upon the spoken Word, we bestow a blessing upon God. It is impossible to bestow a blessing upon the spoken or written Word of God and not upon God himself.

In Psalm 34:1, David says, "I will bestow a blessing on the Lord at all times, and I'm not going to stop praising him." The Greek word for *blessed* is also the same word for *bless*. The difference between these two words is that *blessed* is more of a state of being. It is pretty much what you are. On the other hand, *bless* is pretty much what you do. The definition of *blessed* is geared toward the self, and *bless* is geared toward what you do for others.

In David's case, he is saying "I will Bless the Lord; I will invoke a blessing on the Lord; I will command my soul (Psalm 103: 1). He is saying, "Bless the Lord, O my soul: and all that is within me, bless His holy name." This is an action that David is doing *toward* God.

The Greek definition for *bless* is "to praise, to celebrate with praise" "of that which is addressed to God." David made this statement more than any other statement in his writing. *Bless* means doing to God what God has been doing to you. To really bless God means to give Him something that you have never given before. It is giving Him something that He really loves.

Whenever we praise Him, we are doing what we were created to do. When we bless Him, we are then exercising a godly attribute. We are making a God move on God. We are doing to God what He is doing to us. We are blessing Him!

Blessing God is like sowing a seed. When we sow it, we are owed a harvest. When we bless Him, God owes us a blessing. When we give a blessing, "then it shall be given to us again, measures press down, shaken together, and running over." God will never let us out-bless Him. He will always bless us more than we bless Him. The Greek word for *bless* means "to praise, to celebrate with praise, of that which is addressed to God, to invoke or command." As believers, we can invoke or command blessings toward God through praise.

In at least five psalms, David said, "Bless the Lord oh my soul." There is something about commanding your soul to bless the Lord. David found out that the Lord will, in return, bless the same thing and in the same way that He was blessed. If David's soul blessed the Lord, then the Lord will bless David's soul in return.

Giving God something we have always given Him, like praise, is not the same as giving Him something we have never given Him before.

Giving God praise is standard—that is what we were created to do—but giving Him a blessing is divine.

Like David, we have to search deep down within ourselves and find something we've never found before—or have never given before—and bless Him with it. We can ask the Holy Spirit to help us in our search because the Holy Spirit searches the inward parts to find the deep things that pertain to God.

David said, "I will bless the Lord at all times. When things are good and when things are bad, I will bless Him when I am up and bless Him when I as down. His praises shall continually be in my mouth."

Chapter 5

Blind Bartimaeus's Transition

Jesus, thou son of David, have mercy on me.
—Mark 10:47

A biblical example of transition appears in Mark 10:46–52. Blind Bartimaeus was a beggar on the side of Jericho Road. Jesus was passing by, and Bartimaeus cried out, "Jesus, thou son of David, have mercy on me." The blind man began his transition on Jericho Road.

On the road to Jericho, the season of blindness and begging was coming to an end for Bartimaeus. Addressing Jesus as "thou Son of David" caused Jesus to stand still and call for him to come. Jesus is also calling us to transition. He is telling us it is time to get up from our state of blindness and doing nothing. He's saying, "That is why we are broke and are beggars."

Some people would rather beg than make a transition. Like Bartimaeus, He is calling for us to get up and make a transition. Jesus asked Bartimaeus, "What wilt thou that I should do unto thee?" (Mark 10:51).

Bartimaeus replied, "Lord, that I might receive my sight." He could have said, "I want a car" or "I want a job." Instead, he said, "Give me the thing that I need most: my sight." Bartimaeus specifically told Jesus what he wanted. We all need to be specific in what we want from the Lord and be able to tell him without any reservations or confusion.

Jesus said, "Go thy way; thy faith hath made thee whole." When Jesus said, "Go thy way," He is saying, "Walk in your purpose, walk in your inheritance, pursue your goals, and do it by faith. Even though you don't have your sight yet."

Jesus stated, "Thy faith hath made thee whole." He is saying that "faith comes before sight." Walk by faith, and sight will come. There are a lot of things that we cannot see right now regarding the future, but if we move forward by faith, we will be able to see things more clearly.

"And immediately he (Bartimaeus) received his sight and followed Jesus in the way" (Mark 10:52). After receiving our sight (vision of purpose), we must follow the Word of God and the guidance of the Holy Spirit. This was Bartimaeus's point of transition. This should be our transitioning point when He saves us and calls us to follow Him. After Bartimaeus received his sight, he no longer had to sit and beg. His transition was to follow Jesus.

Waiting for a Transition

The Greek word for *waiting* is *Dechomai*, which means "to wait" or "to expect." This definition indicates that one must wait for a transition—no matter how long it takes. While waiting, one must expect a transition to take place. This is called having faith.

Another Greek word for *waiting* is *Apek*, which means "to wait or expect eagerly," "those who wait" and "represent believers in general, not a section of them." This Greek word indicates that we should not just expect a transition; we should eagerly expect a transition. Eagerly expecting a transition creates a sense of excitement, urgent anticipation, an unwavering anticipation, and anticipation that is hard to get away from. This is the attitude we must have regarding the transition that is on the way.

The Waiting!

One of the most important things regarding Transition is the Waiting. Waiting for a transition can really test your faith. Psalm 30:5 states, "Weeping may endure for a night, but joy cometh in the morning." We know the weeping will be over when morning comes. The waiting for your change or transition will be over. The only problem is the waiting, which we interpret as "the night."

While we are waiting, it is important that we maintain a state of eager expectation regarding our transition. The devil will always attack you during the "night" while you are waiting for your transition. The devil will tell you that you're not going to make it and that all hope is lost. We must stay focused on what the Word of God says. "No weapon formed against us shall prosper," and we are "overcomers in all things."

It's during "the night" (the waiting), that our faith is tested the most. It is important to survive the waiting; otherwise, the transition will be difficult to obtain.

A few things will benefit us while we are waiting. Sometimes, all we can do is wait, especially when we have done all we know how to do. Second, waiting gives you time to reflect on how you got to where you are. Waiting helps you reflect on your life and where you want to go from here. Waiting builds character and develops purpose. Waiting "renews our strength and causes us to mount up with wings as eagles; run and not be weary walk and not faint" (Isaiah 40:31). Waiting strengthens us. Waiting shows God that He can trust you to be patient. James 1:3 states, "The trying of your faith worketh patience." In verse 4, James tells us that we should "let patience have her perfect work, that ye may be perfect and entire, wanting nothing." So having patience completes us to the point that we will be entire and not want for anything.

Initial Transition

Initial transition means where you were before you got to where you are now. The scriptures did not say where Bartimaeus was before he ended up on the side of Jericho Road. Because he was blind, he had to transition to a place that was in the pathway of Jesus. The scriptures did not say how Bartimaeus got there, but he had to get there by some means. He did not receive his sight during the initial transition from where he was before Jericho Road. We have to initially, like Bartimaeus, transition to places where the real manifestation of transition can take place.

We all have to initially get to where we need to be by some means. Initial transition is very rarely seen or known in our own lives because it happens in phases and steps. Most of the time, we don't know why we end up where we are.

This initial transition will always be tested, which probably was true in the case of Bartimaeus, but persistence, faith, and dedication will afford us the benefit of experiencing *transitional manifestation*, which is receiving our sight. Wherever Bartimaeus was before he sat on Jericho Road, he wasn't in the right place for his transition. We have to be in the right place for our transitions too. This may take God putting people in our lives to help with our initial transitions, but God guides all aspects of our transitions.

When a caterpillar goes through metamorphosis (stages of transformation) and grows wings, it first has to be in a place of initial transformation, which is called a cocoon. After metamorphosis (transformation), it has to press or transition its way out of his cocoon. After transitioning its way out of the cocoon, it no longer has to crawl as a caterpillar. After transitioning its way out of the cocoon, it can spread its wings as a butterfly and fly. This flying is also called transition.

Transition Takes Time

> To everything there is a season, and a time to
> every purpose under the heaven.
> —Ecclesiastes 3:1

There is a time for everything and a "season for every purpose." In this scripture, the words for "time" have varied connotations. A period allotted for a special object, task, or cause was "its time." A period of life was "a time." A special period of life was "a time." A period of conception and the days of pregnancy were "a time."

Time, which is *chronos* in Greek, denotes a space of "time," whether it is long or short.

Time doesn't imply "a season." You can have time, but it doesn't mean that it's your season! God will never give you a season without giving you time in that season to do His will. God understands that we need time in our seasons to do His will. Time is allotted to us by Him. It is very important to use the allotted time for His glory and not waste it. Wasted time can never be retrieved.

Time is preciously allotted to us by God. We will have time when we don't have money. To some people, time is money. There will always be a time for everything. We just need find out and know what time it is. Time should always be used wisely because once time is gone, we can never get it back. Wasted time is a wasted opportunity to serve God in our season and in our purpose. Since Ecclesiastes 3:1 states that "there is a time for every purpose," it is time that affords us a purpose in life.

What we do with our time during our purpose is as important as what we do with our purpose during our time. If we waste our time, we also waste our purpose. Purpose can never stop while we are living, and neither does time.

Time waits on no one. While we stand still, time keeps moving. Time will always go on—even when we can't. It is what we do with time that determines our legacy and forges our heritage (our children). Time is a luxury that God has afforded all of us while we are here on earth so that we can accomplish His will and fulfill our purpose. We weren't created for time; time was created for us.

In 2 Timothy 4:6, the apostle Paul stated, "The time of my departure is at hand." Paul was simply saying that it was time for him to leave this world. Paul did not run out of time; he just finished his course and completed his purpose. Time continued to go on long after Paul was gone. There is an allotted time for every purpose; it's what we do with this allotted time that really matters. We can either waste it or take advantage of it.

In Psalm 90:10, Moses stated that "the days of our years are three score years and ten; and if by reason of strength they be four score years." Some people think that when you pass the three score and ten, which is seventy years, that you are living on borrowed time. Having more time than three score and ten is not borrowed time. It is *earned* time, and by grace, it is given. You cannot borrow time; if so, when or how would you pay it back?

When someone asks us what time it is, we can look at our watches or cell phones and chronologically tell them numerically where the hands are, but real time isn't worn on your arm—it is allotted by God.

In Psalm 90:12, Moses states, "Teach us to number our days," which means help us to make good use of our time, according to the time we have at hand, to make plans to fulfill our purpose. According to the guidance to the Holy Spirit, we should do this wisely. That is why we have to be taught.

Moses said, "Teach us." It is not easy to wake up and know what to do with our time; we need to be taught to plan cautiously and not waste our time.

The End of Time

And the angel which I saw stand upon the sea and upon the earth lifted up his hand to heaven, And swear by him that liveth for ever and ever, who created heaven, and the things that therein are, and the earth, and the things that therein are, and the sea, and the things which are therein, that there should be time no longer.

—Revelation 10:5–6

There will come a time when there will be no more time. I can't begin to understand life without time, but I know that life after this will never be the same. The opportunity to complete our seasons will be gone. The opportunity to fulfill our purposes will be gone. The opportunity to do the will of God will be gone.

When "there should be time no longer," things will rapidly take place because there will be no time for the things that depended on time. There will be no more time for humanity. Time would have finally run out or come to an end for humankind. Since time will no longer be a marker, there will be no sense of "whenness." When we do something, there is no more time to do anything else.

Season in Greek is *Kairos*. According to the *Thorndike World Book Dictionary*, it means "the time when something is occurring, active, or at its best, or in fashion."

The Vine's Greek Dictionary states that a "season" is when "The Father has set within His own authority" both the time, the lengths of the periods, and the season." Time, season, and purpose depend on what God the Father has set in His own authority and will.

Seasons, as in the weather, bring forth different environments in the atmosphere and different weather activities. Seasons in our lives are the same; it's a "time when something is occurring, active, or at its best, or in fashion." Seasons are different in a way that things are happening that don't usually happen—like something better happening. When a season is taking place, things seem to just fall into place and work for someone's best interest. Seasons are difficult to understand, and we don't know when they will start or when they will end.

43

A season is just like time—don't waste it! A wasted season also like time because it cannot be retrieved. Whether time or a season, it's what we do with it and in it that really matters.

> For an angel went down at a certain season into the pool, and troubled the water: whosoever then first after the troubling of the water stepped in was made whole of whatsoever disease he had. (John 5:4)

This scripture states that the angel went down at "a certain season." A certain season indicates that this occurrence did not happen every day. There was an opportunity for everyone around the pool to step in and be healed.

There is always a great opportunity when a season comes about. One must always take advantage of that opportunity. In this particular season, you had to be the first one to step into the pool in order to be healed. We must be proactive in our seasons, always waiting to take an urgent step toward success. If not, someone else will beat us to it.

In this scripture, verse 7 states that the man said, "Sir, I have no man, when the water is troubled, to put me into the pool: but while I am coming, another steppeth down before me." We cannot afford to make excuses about why we are not taking advantage of our seasons. One of the easiest things in the world is to blame someone else for our lack of success. When our season comes, we have to take the initiative to take every opportunity and advantage that we can in order to succeed and not make excuses.

Seasons come and go, but a "certain season" is rare. It can be a once-in-a-lifetime thing. We cannot afford to waste it by blaming others for our shortcomings. It is what we do in our season that determines our outcome and success. Someone will always be there to try to block your path, impede your progress, or block your inheritance, but you must put forth the best effort to get to where you want to be and where you need to be. We must not let people hinder or stop us at any point. Stop making excuses—and get up and go forward in your season.

Purpose, which in the Greek is *boulema* or *Bouleuo*, means "take counsel, resolve of oneself, and put or set forth a deliberate intention to do what God created you to do! This means listening to the Holy Spirit, examining ourselves to make sure we are ready and equipped with what we need to fulfill our purpose, and then moving forward in the will of God and doing what God has created us to do.

There is a purpose for everything and everybody. Colossians 3:3 states, "For ye are dead, and your life is hid with Christ in God." This statement indicates that when we are born again, we are dead to the flesh, dead to the sinful nature we once had, and dead to the things of the world. Therefore, your new identity as a Christian is hidden with Christ in God.

Why is it hidden with Christ in God? Anything that is just given to us or is easily found is not always appreciated or taken seriously, but something like a new life or a new identity should be exciting and worth digging for or pursuing. God decided to hide your new life as a Christian so if you really want it, you will be willing to work for it by studying, praying, and following the guidance of the Holy Spirit and the will of God.

The Accuser of Our Brethren

> For the accuser of our brethren is cast down, who accuseth them before our God day and night. And they overcame him because of the blood of the Lamb, and because of the word of their testimony; and they loved not their life even unto death. (Revelation 12:10–11)

Until the devil is cast down, he will continue to accuse the brethren during the day and night. He never sleeps, and he never gets tired. As humans, we take breaks for and from about everything, but the devil never takes a break. As brethren, we must become more consistent in following the will of God and not so prone to taking breaks.

Why Accuse the Brethren?

The devil knows that disobedience in the Word of God brings forth penalties. He also knows that he has the right to accuse the brethren of their disobedience before God the Father. He also knows that he has to get permission from God to carry out punishments for that disobedience if he can rightly accuse the brethren.

Revelation 12:10 states, "For the accuser of our brethren is cast down." There will be a time and a season when the devil will be cast down, and he can no longer accuse the brethren. For now, he never sleeps. He is looking for ways to bring us down, and we must not give him a reason by not fulfilling the will of God.

Verse 11 states, "And they overcame him because of the blood of the Lamb." While the devil is accusing us, we can overcome him by claiming the blood of the lamb and by holding fast to the Word of our testimony, which is continuing to confess the Word of God.

When the devil is successful in accusing the brethren, he can block our blessings and promotions from God.

Chapter 6

Evolving in Transition
(Spiritual Evolution)

Therefore if any man be in Christ, he is a new creature:
old things are passed away; behold, all things are
become new. And all things are of God.
—2 Corinthians 5:17–18

Evolution: (Merriam Webster): (a) A process of change in a certain
direction; (b) A process of continuous change from a lower, simpler,
or worse to a higher, more complex, or better state; (c) a process of
gradual and relatively peaceful social, political, and economic advance.

Salvation (The beginning of Spiritual Evolution)

The Greek word *Metamorphoo* means to be changed into another thing
or creature. A *metamorphosis* is the beginning of spiritual evolution. In 2
Corinthians 5:17, the apostle Paul states, "If any man be in Christ, he is
a new creature" or species, which never existed before. This is spiritual
evolution. The physical body did not change, but the inner man—the
spirit man—did change. He is now a new creature. *Evolution* means "a
process of continuous change, from a lower form of life to a higher form,
to a better state of existence; a gradual process of change."

The difference between the physical evolution and the spiritual
evolution is that the spiritual evolution is all about the spirit of a man
changing and evolving and then the mental, social, political, and economic
advancement that takes place. During this transitional process of change,
we should continue to evolve in every area.

The apostle Paul says, "Old things have passed away, and all things
are new, and all things are of God." The old, sinful nature of man (the old
man) no longer exists. He's done. He died on the cross with Jesus, and the

new nature is the nature of God. Since this scripture says "all things are of God," we know that God is a Spirit and anything from God or of God is also spiritual. The process of spiritual evolution was initiated by God.

> But we all, with open face beholding as in a glass the glory
> of the Lord, are changed into the same image from glory
> to glory, even as by the spirit of the Lord.
> (2 Corinthians 3:18)

The Word of God is the "glass" that reflects the glory of the Lord in who we are in Him. This brings about our transitional change and causes us to spiritually evolve "from glory to glory." This evolving in transition doesn't happen on its own.

We have to show "obedience and faith" by abiding in the Word of God.

> Take my yoke upon you, and learn of me; for my yoke is
> easy, and my burden is light. (Matthew 11:29–30)

> Study to show thyself approved unto God, a workman
> that needeth not to be ashamed, rightly dividing the word
> of truth. (2 Timothy 2:15)

> His delight is in the law of the Lord; and in his law doth
> he meditate day and night, and he shall be like a tree.
> (Psalm 1:2–3)

Evolving in Obedience

What is obedience? The Greek word for *obedience* is *hupakouo*, which means to "to listen, attend," "to submit," and "to obey."

The first part of the Greek word *hupakouo* (hupa) means "under." The latter part of the word, *kouo* means "listen/hear." The Greek word for obedience means "to listen and hear what or who you are subject to or who or what you are under." As believers, we place ourselves under obedience to hear and become doers of the Word of God. Obedience means to listen/hear first, and to be under the law of God's Word and become doers.

Webster's definition of "obedience" is "submissive to the restraint of command of authority or will of another, to comply with the demands or requests of one in authority." This definition reflects the Greek definition of "obedience" by saying that we should submit to the restraint of command of the authority or the will of God's Word to comply with the demands or request of the Word of God.

> Who, (Jesus) being in the form of God, thought it not robbery to be equal with God: But made himself of no reputation, and took upon him the form of a servant, and was made in the likeness of men: And being found in fashion as a man, he humbled himself, and became obedient unto death, even the death of the cross. (Philippians 2:6–8)

This scripture expresses the obedience of Jesus and how He took it upon Himself the form of a servant. Being fashioned as a man, He humbled Himself and became obedient unto death. The definition of obedience is coming under the authority and demands of another.

Jesus humbled Himself under the authority of death and became obedient unto death—even the death on the cross. Obedience is actually the humbling of oneself to do the demands and will of another, which is what Jesus did, and as servants of God the Father, we should humble ourselves to do His will.

Why Is Obedience Important?

Obedience is important because there is a need for God to show us whether or not He can trust us with doing His will—and whether we can be trusted with our own desires and purpose.

God already knows whether He can trust us. God already knows the outcome of what we will do before He trusts us. We are the ones who need convincing. In 1 Samuel 15, King Saul was rejected from being king by the Lord because the Word of the Lord went forth to Saul that he should smite Amalek, utterly destroy all they had, and spare them not. Instead of obeying God, he spared Agag (the king) and took the best of the sheep, oxen, fatlings, lambs, and all that was good, and then he destroyed everything that was vile. When Samuel asked why, Saul told him (verse 19) that it was the people who spared the best of the sheep and the oxen to sacrifice. Saul blamed the people for his lack of obedience as king.

In my first book (*Are You the One?*), I explained why leaders have to be strong, uninfluenced, and obedient in that which God has called, anointed, and appointed them to do. So many times, people who follow leaders will try to influence them in a different direction when it is not the will or the commandment of God.

Leaders who listen to followers will find themselves rejected by the Lord from whatever appointments He has given them. Even though Saul spared King Agag of the Amalekites and the best of the spoils, Samuel called it "evil in the sight of the Lord." This indicates that disobedience is considered evil in the sight of God. When Saul tried to justify his lack of leadership, Samuel responded, "Hath the Lord as great delight in burnt offerings and sacrifices, as in obeying the voice of the Lord?

Obedience is better than sacrifices, and sacrifice can never make up for a lack of obedience. God prefers our obedience to our money and other selfish gifts. A sacrifice or offering without obedience is vain and worthless, and it is considered an act of evil in God's sight. On the other hand, someone who is disobedient will be rejected by the Lord.

> For rebellion is as the sin of witchcraft, and stubbornness is as iniquity and idolatry. Because thou hath rejected the Word of the Lord, He hath also rejected thee from being king. I have sinned: for I have transgressed the commandment of the Lord, and thy words: because I feared the people, and obeyed their voice.
> (1 Samuel 15:23–24)

Leadership appointments are at stake when we do not obey the Word of the Lord.

No matter what level of leadership you have, if you're not obedient, your work is in vain. To be appointed as king without being disciplined in obedience is vain. Obedience is the best way to learn and receive from God.

A person must be disciplined before obedience can be applied. There is nothing to obey if you have not been disciplined.

> Whosoever hearth these sayings of mine, and doeth them, I will liken him unto a wise man, which built his house upon a rock: and the rain descended, and the floods came, and the winds blew, and beat upon that house; and it fell not; for it was founded upon a rock. (Matthew 7:24–25)

Obedience is doing what you hear. Jesus is saying that a wise man learns how to stand by being obedient to what he hears.

> Ye have not chosen me, but I have chosen, you, and ordained you, that ye should go and bring forth fruit, and that your fruit should remain: that whatsoever ye shall ask of the father in my name, he may give it you. (John 15:16)

Jesus is saying, "I have chosen you, and I have prepared (ordained) you for this appointment. The appointment is to go and bring forth fruit, and that your fruit should remain."

God's Word says that our obedience actually causes our fruit to remain. However, if we don't keep our appointment by way of obedience, our fruit might stand for a while. A lack of obedience can put us and our followers in positions of devastation, including fruit that is in obedience to His Word.

"If the blind lead the blind, then both will end up in the ditch." Jesus ended verse 16 by saying, "That whatever you ask the Father in Jesus's name," He would do it. Obedience puts a great demand on the Father concerning the covenant we have with Him. According to our covenant with the Father, if we do what we are supposed to do, He will honor His part and give us what we want, need, or desire.

Obedience is just one of the major factors that allow God to move on our behalf.

Obedience unto Death

> He humbled himself, and became obedient unto
> death, even the death of the cross.
> —Philippians 2

> For as by one man's disobedience many were made sinners, so
> by the obedience of one shall many be made righteous.
> —Romans 5:19

Adam was the first man who was given the responsibility of obeying God, and because he failed to do so, sin passed on to all humankind. Adam was ordained of God to be prince of this world, but when he disobeyed God and obeyed Satan, he lost his title as prince of this world—and it was forfeited (passed on) to Satan. God did not reject Adam; Adam willingly yielded to obey Satan and gave up his title by his act of disobedience.

The first king of Israel (Saul) was rejected because of his disobedience.

> He (Jesus) humbled himself, and became obedient unto
> death, even the death of the cross. (Philippians 2:6)

Jesus was obedient to the Father during the course of his life—and all the way to His death. After Jesus met up with death, He had to humble Himself. If he had not, death could not have taken Him.

Jesus knew what He had to do. He said that He can lay His life down when He was ready, and no one could take it. In order for death to take Him, He had to humble Himself and give in to death. What great obedience Jesus exercised by giving in to death! He obeyed death, and He also obeyed torment, pain, and humiliation.

Some might say He took His own life, but He didn't. He surrendered to death by saying, "Father into thy hands I commend my spirit." Jesus's example of obedience afforded people righteousness with God and the right to the nature of God (Romans 5:19). Like Jesus, we have to be obedient so people can be led to righteousness—and so that God can accomplish His will in our lives on earth.

God's perfect will is His permissive will (1 Samuel 8:10–22). God's Word should be good enough, but sometimes it is not enough to tell us through His Word what is or is not His will. God allows us to go through and play out the drama of His permissive will, which in Saul's case included rejection of being king.

Obedience Earns God's Respect and Trust

If we abide by the Word of God and if the Word of God abides in us, we can ask what our will is and our desires are, and it shall be done unto us (John 15:7). Being obedient in abiding by God's Word earns us respect and trust of God. He will give us whatever we want and desire. If we delight ourselves in the Lord, the Word says He shall give us the desires of our hearts.

Obedience is important because it is the perfect will of God. From the foundation of the world, we have been called, chosen, adopted, and predestined to walk in all that God has already planned for us in His perfect will. Obedience is walking in the perfect will of God. This is also how God directs us in our purpose.

God's permissive will—not His perfect will—allows us to act out and have what we want. In advance, we really don't know what we will do in certain circumstances. God already knows what we will do, but God allows us to see what we would do and whether or not He can trust us. When we fail in God's permissive will, we will know why God didn't want us to have a certain thing in the first place—and if He can or cannot trust us.

The final reason why obedience is important is explained in Isaiah 1:19–20: "If ye be willing and obedient; ye shall eat the good of the land, But if ye refuse and rebel, ye shall be devoured with the sword (the Word of God).

Exercising our will to obey the will and the Word of God earns the benefit of enjoying and eating of the good of the land. On the other hand, not obeying the will and the Word of God causes us to be devoured with the same Word that we disobeyed, which shall be a sword of destruction: "For the mouth of the Lord hath spoken it."

> For as by one man's disobedience many were made sinners,
> so by the obedience of one shall many be made righteous.
> (Romans 5:19)

This scripture is talking about how Adam's disobedience caused all humankind to enter into sin, but by the obedience of Jesus, humankind was moved unto righteousness.

> Know ye not, that to whom ye yield yourselves servants to
> obey, his servants ye are to whom ye obey; whether of sin
> unto death, or of obedience unto righteousness? But God
> be thanked, that we were the servants of sin, but ye have
> obeyed from the heart that form of doctrine which was
> delivered you. Being then made free from sin, ye became
> the servants of righteousness. (Romans 6:16–18)

When you yield your body or your mind to obey and serve sin, the devil or our own fleshly desires—whatever we choose to serve—becomes our master. Whether sin unto death or obedience unto righteousness, this behavior brings forth death or life.

> For though we walk in the flesh, we do not war after the
> flesh: For the weapons of our warfare are not carnal, but
> mighty through God to the pulling down of strongholds;
> Casting down imaginations and every high thing that
> exalteth itself against the knowledge of God, and bringing
> into captivity every though to the obedience of Christ.
> (2 Corinthians 10:3–6)

These scriptures let us know that it is our responsibility to pull down any and every thought and stronghold that competes against the Word of God. We should pull them down from our minds and imaginations by studying and meditating on the Word of God instead of entertaining carnal thoughts.

The second part of this scripture lets us know that we have the power through Christ Jesus to bring into captivity every thought to the obedience of Christ. Obedience is something that we can exercise through the Word of God when it comes to pulling down the exalted and high things against God's Word.

Verse 6 is talking about "having in a readiness to revenge all disobedience, when your obedience is fulfilled." It takes obedience to fulfill obedience and avenge disobedience. It takes obedience in studying the Word of God to obey the Word of God, and at the same time, it takes obedience to avenge disobedience. It takes obedience to say to disobedience, "You are wrong!" No one likes to admit they are wrong or tell someone else they are wrong, but it takes obedience to avenge disobedience.

> And if any man obey not our word by this epistle, note that man, and have no company with him, that he may be ashamed. Yet count him not as an enemy, but admonish him as a brother. (2 Thessalonians 3:14–15)

When I first read this scripture, I thought it was being a little hard on anyone who did not obey the Word of God. If not obeying the Word is the same as being cursed, I understand now that no one likes being part of another man's curse. When you share the company of a cursed person, you share or take company with the curse itself. We don't have to share the company of a disobedient person. Instead, pray for them and count them as misguided brothers.

Abiding by the Word of God is an act of faith and obedience, but this is only one part of spiritual evolution in our transition. The other part is becoming active and doing what the Word of God says.

> But whoso looketh into the perfect law of liberty, and continueth therein, he being not a forgetful hearer, but "a doer" of the work, this man shall be blessed in his deeds. (James 1:25)

This verse lets us know that we have to become doers in order to evolve into our blessings. Actually, being a doer of what the Word of God says causes us to develop and spiritually evolve.

Chapter 7

Evolving in Transition
(Evolving through Suffering)

Though he were a son, yet learned he obedience
by the thing which he suffered.
—Hebrews 5:8

The last part of evolving in transition is evolving through suffering and afflictions. The Greek word for *suffer* is *hupomeno*. This word means hardship, trouble, need, want, loss, persecution, or shipwreck.

This definition lets us know that suffering is a result of "hardship and trouble." Being in need causes suffering; to be in want causes suffering; to lose something or to be persecuted and shipwreck all causes suffering. Suffering is not just a state of being; it is also an emotional feeling. Suffering causes a person to be imprisoned in a state of being.

There are many reasons why we suffer. In *Why? Because You Are Anointed,* T. D. Jakes states that one of the main reasons that Christians suffer is because of the anointing. "It is without exception, absolutely necessary for the anointed to suffer." Jakes adds, "Also you have to know that just as God has promised to supply all our needs according to His riches in glory, He also has promised us trials and tribulations in this life. Tribulations and trials serve, by the aid of the Holy Spirit, a divine purpose." Jake goes on to state that divine purpose is "death." That death, Jake states, is to the flesh. Jakes states, "If you are going to walk in the anointing and presence of God, you must be dead to self." In reading these statements, I have come to the conclusion that suffering causes us to die to the flesh.

The apostle Paul states that we need to "present our bodies a living sacrifice" and that we should bring it under subjection to the Word of God because there is a law in the flesh that brings us into bondage. "Though he were a son, yet learned he obedience by the thing which he suffered" (Hebrews 5:8).

Some things are learned only by suffering. Jesus didn't have to suffer to learn. By the age of twelve, He had already learned enough to consult with the scribes and lawyers of his day. Jesus chose to suffer because He wanted to set an example for us that suffering teaches us a hard lesson, builds character, and allows us to share in His glory.

> If we suffer with Him we are also glorified with Him.
> For I reckon that the suffering of this present time are
> not worthy to be compared with the glory which shall be
> revealed in us. (Romans 8:17–18)

In other words, the payoff, which is His revealed glory in us, will be greater than the pain and suffering that we are going through now; there will be no comparison.

Sometimes we get caught up in the pain of suffering and forget about the glory that shall be revealed because of the suffering. If we focus on the glory more that the pain, "then the light affliction and suffering won't last but for a moment" (2 Corinthians 4:17–18).

First Peter 4:13 states that we should "rejoice in as much as ye are partakers of Christ's sufferings; that, when his glory shall be revealed, ye may be glad also with exceeding joy." In other words, instead of displaying pain and feeling behind the suffering for Christ's sake, we should rejoice so that when His glory is revealed, we can feel exceeding joy. Revelation and manifested glory always bring gladness and exceeding joy.

> Most gladly therefore will I rather glory in my infirmities,
> that the power of Christ may rest upon me. Therefore I
> take pleasure in infirmities, in reproaches, in necessities,
> in persecutions, in distresses for Christ's sake: for when
> I am weak, then am I strong. (2 Corinthians 12:9b, 10)

Paul is experiencing afflictions and infirmities, but he chooses to glorify or rejoice so that the power of Christ may rest upon him. Paul is saying, "The more I glorify and rejoice, the more powerful I become in

Christ. I have learned to take pleasure in anything that is negative so that when I am weak, I am made strong."

> For as the sufferings of Christ abound in us, so our consolation also aboundeth by Christ. And whether we be afflicted, it is for your consolation and salvation, which is effectual in the enduring of the same sufferings which we also suffer: or whether we be comforted, it is for your consolation and salvation. And our hope of you is steadfast, knowing, that as ye are partakers of the sufferings, so shall ye be also of the consolation. (2 Corinthians 1:5–7)

The more we suffer for the sake of Christ, the more we are comforted by Christ.

> For what glory is it, if when ye be buffeted for your faults, ye shall take it patiently? But if, when ye do well and suffer for it, ye take it patiently, this is acceptable with God. (1 Peter 2:20–21)

It is far better to suffer for doing well than for doing badly. First of all, this is acceptable with God; secondly, by doing badly, there is no glory behind the suffering.

> For even hereunto were ye called: because Christ also suffered for us, leaving us an example, that ye should follow his steps. (1 Peter 2:21)

Jesus did not have to suffer. He did not sin, and Jesus owed us nothing. But for the sake of setting an example of associating suffering with glory, He did it for us, "leaving an example that we should follow in His steps:"

In Philippians 3:10, the apostle Paul states that in order to "know Him, and the power of His resurrection, and the fellowship of His sufferings, being made conformable unto His death:"

The true order of this scripture is first getting to know Him by studying his Word. The next thing is fellowshipping with His sufferings, which will build character, patience, and long-suffering. After we suffer and die to the flesh and the self, we experience the power of His resurrection. You can't resurrect until you die.

The power of His resurrection is basically experiencing the process of evolving from death because we can't stay dead; we have to get up and evolve. We must evolve from dead works, dead habits, dead attitudes, and dead behaviors to a newness in Christ Jesus.

> Humble yourselves therefore under the mighty hand of God, that he may exalt you in due time. Casting all your care upon him; for he careth for you. Be sober, be vigilant; because your adversary the devil, as a roaring lion, walketh about, seeking whom he may devour whom resist steadfast in the faith, knowing that the same afflictions are accomplished in your brethren that are in the world. but the God of all grace, who hath called us unto his eternal glory by Christ Jesus, after that ye have suffered a while, make you perfect, stablish, strengthen, settle you. (1 Peter 5:6–10)

Humility plays a big role in our spiritual evolution, and exaltation from God indicates promotion and a higher level, which is indicated in the definition of evolution, but it all starts with humility.

Suffering is not what causes you to evolve; it is you using the suffering as a catalyst to build character and become "perfect, establish, strengthen, and settled." What also causes us to evolve is standing on the Word of God and resisting the devil. God will use our circumstances of suffering to work together for our good, and He will cause us to evolve from it.

In *The Purpose Driven Life*, Rick Warren states that God uses circumstances to develop our character. He depends more on circumstances to make us like Jesus than He depends on us reading the Bible. You face circumstances twenty-four hours per day, Warren says, and your most profound and intimate experiences of worship will likely be in your darkest days—when your heart is broken, when you feel abandoned, when you're out of options, when the pain is great—and you turn to God alone.

During suffering, we learn to pray our most authentic, heartfelt, honest-to-God prayers. God could have kept Joseph out of jail, Daniel out of the lion's den, Jeremiah out of the slime pit, Paul from being shipwrecked three times, and the three Hebrew boys out of the furnace, but He didn't. He allowed those problems to happen, and each of them was drawn closer to God as a result.

There are four things we have to do in order to evolve through our suffering:

- Verse 7: "Cast your all care upon Him, for He careth for you."
- Verse 8: "Be sober."
- Verse 9: "Whom resist steadfast in the faith."
- Verse 10: Encourage yourself by "knowing that the same afflictions are accomplished in your brethren that are in the world."

Several types of lizards are able to escape an enemy's grasp by breaking off part of their own tails. The tail has a weak spot just for this purpose. If a predator grabs the lizard by its tail, the tail easily comes off. It can grow back over time, but it won't look quite the same. That is better than being someone else's dinner. The lizard would rather suffer the loss of its tail than the loss of its life. Like the lizard, we must suffer the loss of some things in order to persevere through the greater things. God is able to grow back and replace the things we have lot. He can even make us better and stronger. Job lost everything, but he regained everything he lost and more.

Chapter 8

Evolving from Feelings and Emotions

For we have not a high priest that cannot be
touched with the feeling of our infirmities.
—Hebrews 4:14–16

Feelings can be deceiving. What you feel can very much be real, especially when it comes to pain, but everything you feel isn't always necessarily the way things are. The pain may be serious, but the reason behind it might not be. Until the feelings and symptoms are diagnosed, it is just an unknown feeling.

Feelings can be deceiving because they can change from one moment to the next. If your life is based on feelings, it will continuously be changing from moment to moment. Just because someone feels lost, it doesn't mean that they are. It is a biblical fact that Jesus came into our hearts and brought salvation to our souls—whether we feel like it or not. And just because we feel lonely, it doesn't mean we are alone.

Jesus stated that He would never leave us or forsake us—and that He will be with us always, even until the end of the world. A lot of the time, feeling lonely is just a feeling. Feelings can be deceiving, especially when the devil exploits them and uses them to his advantage.

Thoughts can also be deceiving. The things we think about are not always correct or true. Some thoughts are just suggestions that are shot into our heads by the fiery darts of the enemy. If we dwell on these thoughts, they play into our feelings and hold us hostage to these thoughts and feelings. We become prisoners to our own feeling and thoughts. This is how the enemy exploits our emotions to his benefit. Once a thought or a feeling is given birth to, it is difficult to abort.

> For we have not a high priest that cannot be touched with
> the feeling of our infirmities. (Hebrews 4:14–16)

Jesus can be touched with our infirmities, and He can be touched by how they feel. When we hurt, He also feels our pain.

The Greek word for *feeling* is *sumpatheo*, which means "to have a fellow-feeling for or with," or "to have compassion." We get our English words *sympathetic* and *sympathy* from this word. This means that Jesus is our High Priest. While feeling what we feel, He becomes sympathetic and shows sympathy toward our feelings. This is why He implores us to "come boldly to the throng of grace and obtain mercy and fine grace to help in time of need." (Hebrews 4:16)

Feelings are real. Feelings happen when the mind, the emotions, or the body is stimulated by attacks of the enemy. In *Let It Go*, Tony Evan states, "Our emotions are particularly vulnerable to satanic attack because emotions are feelings that have no intellect of their own." He adds, "Emotional strongholds are attitudes that result in actions that hold a person hostage to something contrary to the will of God. But strongholds are feelings or actions that dominate your life and consume most of your time and effort."

The devil knows how to exploit our weak areas with negative attacks and assault on our character, finances, marriages, and bodies. Some other negative things he uses are gossip, lies, physical abuse, and emotional abuse.

Tony Evan states, "For many Christians, the cause of their emotional trauma is not the emotions themselves. It is because they have not understood their true identity in Christ or learned to live by grace—so they don't know how to respond to the spiritual causes of their attitudinal distresses."

The purpose of these negative attacks is to take us out of character, and when we have been taken out of character, the second line of attack will be the feelings of guilt, shame, and condemnation. The most prevalent assault is on our minds. "For as he thinketh in his heart, so is he" (Proverbs 23:7).

We often respond to the things that we are thinking, which is called becoming a product or victim of one's thoughts. If the enemy can attack our minds and make us feel defeated, we will begin to act and behave defeated.

How to Deal with Feelings

To start dealing with feelings, we have to change the way we think. We have to stop being susceptible to negative attacks on our minds, and this is done by obtaining a spiritual mind: "Let this mind be in you which was also in Christ Jesus" (Philippians 2:5). It is part of our inheritance to have a spiritual mind; all we have to do is program our minds with the Word of God every chance we get. When we program our minds with the Word of God, it blocks the attacks of the enemy.

> Whatsoever things are true, whatsoever things are honest, whatsoever things are just, whatsoever are pure, whatsoever things are lovely, whatsoever things are of good report; if there be any virtue, and if there be any praise, think on these things. (Philippians 4:8)

"Think on these things" means not thinking about your problems or anything else that is contrary to the will and the Word of God.

Philippians 4:8 gives us a list of spiritual virtues that will keep and protect our minds if we think and meditate on them.

One of the main ways to deal with feelings is by "casting down imaginations, and every high thing that exalted itself against the knowledge of God, and bringing into captivity every thought to the obedience of Christ" (2 Corinthians 10:5).

The understood subject in this verse is "you." Casting down imaginations that the enemy has propped up in our minds is a responsibility that we all must take upon ourselves. It is not just imaginations or thoughts; it is every high thing, like emotional feelings of guilt, shame, or condemnation. Cast them down by using the Word of God and what God's Word says about these problems.

Romans 12:2 states that we can be "transformed by the renewing of our mind" in the Word of God. When our minds are renewed in and by the Word of God, our entire lives can be transformed.

To deal with feelings we have to also be like David: "But his delight is in the law of the Lord; and his law doth he meditate day and night" (Psalm 1:2). When facing problems and dealing with feelings, we have to constantly meditate the Word of God day and night because the enemy never stops or sleeps.

We need to meditate day and night until we become "like a tree planted by the rivers of water, that bringeth forth his fruit in his season; his leaf also shall not wither, and whatsoever he doeth shall prosper" (Psalm 1:3). A tree that bringeth forth its fruit in its season denotes a mature tree. This scripture is also saying that meditating on the Word of God brings you to a mature state of being.

The Most Important Part about Dealing with Feelings

The most important thing about dealing with feelings is remembering who we are and remembering what we have. We, as believers, have so much to our advantage in who we are in Christ and what we have in our inheritance.

> We are lively stones, are built up a spiritual house, an holy priesthood, to offer up spiritual sacrifices, acceptable to God by Jesus Christ. (1 Peter 2:5)

We are part of Christ and part of a "spiritual house," which means we are not by ourselves. Our lives are made up of many parts that support the entire house.

> But ye are a chosen generation, a royal priesthood, an holy nation, a peculiar people; that ye should shew forth praises of Him who called us out of Darkness into His marvelous light. 1 (Peter 2:9)

This verse tells us that we are a "holy priesthood," a "chose generation," and a "royal priesthood." Throughout the Old Testament, we were aware of the holy priesthood and the royalty of kingship, but they are not seen in one body until Jesus.

As he saith also in another place, "Thou art a priest for ever after the order of Melchizedek." (Hebrews 5:6)

Melchizedek was a king and a priest: "For this Melchizedek, king of Salem, priest of the most high God (Hebrews 7:1). According to Hebrews 5:6, Jesus was after the same order as Melchizedek.

If we are in Christ Jesus, we to are "a royal priesthood," which means holy nation. Since Melchizedek was a priest and a king (1 Peter 2:9), we carry the same authority of a royal king as Christ and in Christ.

Paul states that we are crucified with Christ (Galatians 2:20). Ephesians 2:6 states, "And hath raised us up together, and made us sit together in heavenly places in Christ Jesus." In this verse, "together" and "us" were stated twice, which means that special emphasis is on "us" and "together" to denote our authority in Christ and with Christ. We are seated with Him in the same seat of authority as a king and a priest after the order of Melchizedek. This is why we are permitted to enter the holy of holies as a royal priesthood and "come boldly to the throne of grace and obtain mercy and fine grace to help us in times of need."

> In time past were not a people, but are now the people of God: which had not obtained mercy, but now have obtained mercy. (1 Peter 2:10)

In Philippians 3:10, Paul stated that we are "in fellowship with Christ's suffering." He understands our sufferings, and He feels what we feel. He felt them in the Garden of Gethsemane when He looked into the cup of His future and our future. He felt what we felt losing a loved one at the tomb of Lazarus. "Then Jesus wept." He felt what they felt.

On the cross, He felt what we should have felt.

> He was wounded for our transgressions, bruised for our iniquities: the chastisement of our peace was upon him; and with his stripes we are healed. (Isaiah 53:5)

He died and rose again, sitting on the right hand of the Father, making intercessions for us as the Great High Priest. We are the little priests. Because we are one with His suffering and fellowship, He feels what we feel. Therefore, He can be touched with our feelings. All we have to do is go boldly to His throne of grace and find mercy and grace to help us in our times of need.

Encouraging Yourself

And David was greatly distressed; for the people spake of stoning him, because the soul of all the people was grieved, every man for his sons and for his daughters: but David encouraged himself in the Lord his God.
—1 Samuel 30:6

In life, bad things will happen—and it might look like your fault. First of all, everything happens for a reason, and it is not necessarily your fault.

Don't let guilt and blame from yourself or other people consume you. The devil always uses guilt and blame against Christians, especially when they don't understand why their problem is happening. Blame and guilt can be very effective weapons.

Martha said to Jesus, "If you had been here, my brother would not have died." (John 11:21)

Whether Jesus wept out of blame or guilt, the shortest verse in the Bible, verse 35, states that "Jesus wept." Sometimes guilt and blame can really hurt. Guilt and blame can darken your perception or put you on the defense. When someone becomes defensive, it takes that person out of godly character and focus. Staying focused is something that the Word of God encourages us to do because we need to depend on the Word when there is no one there to encourage us.

There comes a time when we all, by way of encouragement, "urge ourselves forward." This is something we have to do when no one else will. *Paraklesis* means "a calling to one's aid" (*para*, "by the side," *Kaleo*, to call") by a Paraclete or an advocate." This definition lets us know that we are not alone or by ourselves. When we need encouragement, the presence of God will be with us, encouraging us or calling us to encouragement.

We have to urge ourselves forward by whatever means necessary. Philippians 3:13a states, "This one thing I do forgetting the things which are behind me." We must put our faults and mistakes behind us. Dragging the past with us only keeps us in the shadows of the past, and we can never move forward. We must try to forget the things that are behind us before we "reach forth unto those things which are before us" (Philippians 3:13b).

In Philippians 3:14, Paul states, "I press." I urge myself forward. I am moving by faith—even though I don't feel like it and in spite of what people are saying. I can't stand still. I must keep moving.

There will come times when things look bad, and you won't know what to do. Everybody you know has disappeared, and all the people you were there for when they needed you are no longer there for you. Your body might be in pain, you might not have the money to pay your bills, or the mental pressure could be more than you can bear.

We have to encourage ourselves. We have to tell ourselves that we are better than where we are. We know we can do better than this. We have to stop feeling down. We have to stop crying and get up from here. Weeping may have endured for the night, but now it's morning—and joy is here.

Tell yourself that this weapon of guilt and blame that the devil has formed against you cannot prosper because there is a Paraclete in my situation. I am not by myself in this thing. I am on my way up and on my way out. This too shall pass. If God is for me—it is more than the whole world against me. I thank God for giving me the victory.

PART III

Tranquility
(Peace, Quiet, Rest)

Chapter 9

What is Tranquility
(Peace, Quiet, Rest)

Thou wilt keep him in perfect peace, whose mind is
stayed on thee: because he trusteth in thee.
—Isaiah 26:3

What is Tranquility?

The *World Book Dictionary* defines "tranquility or peace" as "a harmonious relationship between two (man and God) accomplished through the Gospel; the sense of rest and contentment."

Merriam Webster states that "tranquil or tranquility" means to be "free from agitation of mind or spirit" or "free from disturbance or turmoil." This can only be accomplished through the Word of God.

The World Book Dictionary definition means that a person has to be born again and become a Christian in order to obtain this type of "tranquility or peace." The relationship between humans and God can only be accomplished through the Gospel.

The first Greek word for tranquility is *hesuchios,* which means "tranquility rising from within, causing no disturbance to others." This type of tranquility or peace suggests having an inner peace or quietness within oneself. Most people desire inner peace and tranquility, but in this changing world, it is difficult to obtain without Jesus Christ.

When many people are disturbed, this emotion results in disturbing others. A person with inner tranquility and peace in Christ can help others find that same peace. Even though their minds are disturbed—and their environments are disturbing—with the peace of Christ "that passes all understanding," it can "keep their hearts and minds." This peace "rises from within" and can only be obtained through the Word of God and a relationship with Him through Jesus Christ.

71

Having peace as a Christian does not mean we will not be disturbed; on the contrary, having peace makes us a target for the enemy. The enemy's main priority is to disturb our peace. Having peace, although being a target of the enemy or being disturbed by the enemy, allows us the benefit of not being moved or taken out of character. There will be multiple attacks of the enemy, but God promised to keep us in perfect peace if our minds stay on Him.

"Therefore whosoever heareth these sayings of mine, and doth them, I will liken him unto a wise man, which built his house upon a rock" (Matthew 7:24). Our sanctuary of peace is the rock in this scripture that the man built his house upon. Peace is our unshakable and unmovable foundation that we become and that we have in our Christian lives.

> And the rain descended, and the floods came, and the winds blew, and beat upon that house; and it fell not: for it was founded upon a rock. (Matthew 7:25)

Peace gives us stability in our lives; that stability will be attacked, but it's not going anywhere. The peace of God that passes all understanding allows us the opportunity to survive any storm that comes our way. Being a doer of the Word strengthens our foundation and helps build a stronger life in Christ. This is the result of having peace. This is what peace means to us. Our job is to obtain peace; God's job is to perfect that peace and keep us in it (Isaiah 26:3).

> And everyone who hears these words of mine and does not do them, will be like a foolish (stupid) man who build his house on the sand. And the rain fell, and the floods and torrents came, and the winds blew and slammed against that house; and it fell—and great was the fall of it. (Matthew 7:26)

Some might say the foolish man who built his house on the sand did not have the opportunity to build his house on a rock as the wise man did, but I think it is fair to say that some people like to make excuses for they don't do the things they should do because of a lack of opportunity or substance. God the Father gave all His children equal opportunities to make choices on how, where, and what to build their lives on. If He didn't, He would not be a just and fair God.

Some people just choose the wrong things when it comes to spiritual guidance and advice. This is what Matthew 7:26 calls building your house on sand. Sand is unsettling and unstable; it is very shifty and movable when it comes to strong winds and storms. That's why it is not a good idea to build your house on sand. The Bible calls this behavior "foolish" or "stupid."

Sand represents anything in life that is not trustworthy, stable, or sure; sometimes trusting people or situations can become like building on sand. The foolish man heard the same words of Jesus that the wise man heard, but he decided not to follow the advice or instructions; therefore, suffered a great fall.

Peace is the rock and the foundation that the foolish man should have built his house on. Peace gives us the stability that we need to survive the storm. A strong wind or storm can shake any building; life can be shaken by many things, but the most important thing is not to fall. Even if we fall, we are still able to get back up with God's help. "A righteous or a wise man can fall seven times and still get back up" (Proverbs 24:16).

The second Greek word for tranquility is *anapausis,* which means "rest" or "to cease." Christ's "rest" is not a "rest from work. It is a rest *in* work, not the ceasing from activity but of the harmonious working of all the faculties and affections. The will, heart, imagination, and conscience are found in God, which is the ideal sphere for its satisfaction and development.

How Do We Obtain Tranquility?

Rest

The Greek word for rest is *anapausis,* a rest in work, not ceasing from activity, but of the harmonious working of all the faculties and affections. "Come unto me, all ye that labor (work) and are heavy laden, and I will give you rest" (Matthew 11:28).

The work of ministry can be very taxing. It can take a toll on you spiritually, mentally, and physically. After a while, you find yourself tired and drained and in need of rest. Even Jesus "went to sleep in the hinder part of ship" (Mark 4:38). When people go to sleep between ministerial appointments, they are tired and drained. Rest is needed to recuperate the body.

> For we wrestle not against flesh and blood, but against
> principalities, against powers, against the rulers of the
> darkness of this world, against spiritual wickedness in
> high places. (Ephesians 6:12)

Dealing with spiritual wickedness in high places can drain you spiritually. It can drain your faith. Rest is often needed to continue to battle against the dark forces and spiritual wickedness of this world.

> Take my yoke upon you and learn of me, for I am meek
> and lowly in heart: and ye shall fine rest unto your souls.
> (Matthew 11:29)

Rest for the soul is the mind or intellect. The soul, mind, and intellect need rest in labor and not from labor. The body needs rest from labor because when you sleep, you're not working. That is when you're resting.

Taking the yoke of Jesus upon you indicates that Jesus will help you obtain a place of rest. In biblical times, oxen and cows would often be yoked together with wooden slabs across their necks. This yoking together helped lessen the strain on the animals during the work. Jesus is saying, "Take my yoke upon you and together we can fine rest while doing the work."

Taking the yoke of Jesus upon you means inviting the Word of God into your daily routine and allowing the Holy Spirit to guide you through your ministerial journey. Jesus will always be yoked together with you. This is that "harmonious working relationship between God and man that the Greek word anapausis defines.

Peace

The same Greek word that defines "rest" also defines "peace" (anapausis). These two words have one thing in common: "a harmonious working relationship between two (God and man)." *The World Book Dictionary* states that this relationship is "accomplished through the Gospel."

In 1 Corinthians 7:15, Paul states, "God hath called us to peace." We all have a calling on our spiritual lives to peace, and we also know that the calling of the Lord is "without repentance" (Romans 11:29). This statement indicates that the call to peace is irreversible. God will not resend it. It belongs to us because of our covenant with Him. "He is our peace" (Ephesians 2:14).

In John 14:27, Jesus said, "Peace I leave with you, my peace I give unto you; not as the world gives, give I unto you." The peace that Jesus leaves with us is not like the peace that the world has, which is temporary peace. Temporary peace is peace that lasts only while and when you're not disturbed or while your life is not disrupted. When your life is disturbed or disrupted, temporary peace becomes temporary. The peace that Jesus gave us is eternal peace in everything.

The devil wants to disturb your peace by disturbing your harmonious relationship with Jesus. If the enemy can compromise your peace, he can also compromise your relationship with Jesus. He can disturb your faith and cause you to begin to doubt and unbelieve. Without faith, it is impossible to please God.

Getting something from God can be very difficult without faith. The enemy can use anything to disturb your peace. He can use jobs, friends, sickness, money problems, distress, and many other things to disturb your peace.

Quiet

There are two Greek words for "quiet." The first is *eremos*, which means "quiet, tranquil." It indicates tranquility arising from without. The second Greek word for "quiet" is *hesuchios*, which means the same as the first definition, but instead of tranquility arising from without, "it is arising from within." Eremos indicates outside or environmental tranquility, and hesuchios indicates inside or internal tranquility. Both of these Greek words represent the word "quiet."

The truth about "quiet," compared to "peace and rest," is that one can be quiet but not have peace or be at rest. Being quiet does not imply peace or rest. Some of the quietest folks in the world are some of the most dangerous folks. You never know what they are thinking. Quiet helps initiate peace and rest because before you can have peace or be at rest, you have to be quiet.

Another definition of quiet is to be still.

Chapter 10

Why Tranquility?
(Peace, Quiet, Rest)

Thou wilt keep him in perfect peace, whose mind is stayed on thee:
because he trusteth in thee.
—Isaiah 26:3

When you're at peace or have peace, the attacks of the enemy is less because peace becomes a strong standard in your life against the enemy. Secondly, peace helps you stay focus on the important things in life, mainly the Word of God. Having peace affords you the opportunity to hear the voice of God clearer and better.

Having peace puts a demand on your inheritance, your exaltation and promotion from God. Peace in your life shows God that you are mature enough to receive these things.

But seek ye first the kingdom of God and his righteousness;
and all these things shall be added unto you.
(Matthew 7:33)

Perfect Peace

Thou wilt keep him in perfect peace, whose mind is
stayed on thee: because he trusteth in thee.
—Isaiah 26:3

"Perfect peace" is defined as "a harmonious working relationship between God and man" and a "wholistic or well-rounded or complete" harmonious relationship between two (God and man), which is accomplished through the Gospel with the sense of rest and contentment. The words *wholistic, well-rounded,* and *complete* are the key.

Perfect peace doesn't mean peace without flaws; it means complete peace in every area of life. The word "perfect" means complete and wholistic. Life isn't complete or whole when you have plenty of money but are physically sick all the time. Life isn't complete or whole when you have plenty of money, and your marriage is bad. Perfect peace is when every area of your life is doing well by the grace of God.

In Matthew 11:29, Jesus says "Take my yoke upon you, and learn of me; for I am meek and lowly in heart: and ye shall find rest unto your souls." We have concluded that rest is obtained through Jesus Christ by taking His yoke (the Word of God) upon you. Learning of me is accomplished by studying the Word of God and by doing what the Word says. David said, "In thy word do I meditate day and night" (Psalm 1).

We, as believers, have to study the Word of God and meditate in it day and night until we become a fully grown tree by the rivers of water—the living waters of God's Word. Meditation is of the mind; when we meditate on the Word of God, this is "keeping our mind stayed on him" (Isaiah 26:3). This is how we maintain "perfect peace." God promises to keep us in this perfect peace if we keep our minds on His Word.

How Do We Keep Our Minds?

Philippians 2:5 states, "Let this mind be in you, which was also in Christ Jesus." The mind of Christ in available to us, and all we have to do is "let it be in us." When you let something be in you, you have to make a conscious decision to do whatever is necessary for it to be there.

Philippians 4:7–9 states, "And the peace of God, which passeth all understanding, shall keep your hearts and minds through Christ Jesus." The peace of God is that harmony we have with God through Jesus Christ (the Word).

Philippians 4:8 goes on to tell us how we keep our minds:

> Finally, brethren, whatsoever things are true, whatsoever things are honest, whatsoever things are just, whatsoever things are pure, whatsoever things are lovely, whatsoever things are of good report; if there be any virtue, and if there be any praise, think on these things.

If we are to maintain our peace and keep our focus, we have to practice these things in the Word of God. Proverbs 23:7 says, "For as he thinketh in his heart, so is he:" As we abide in the Word, we become a product of whatever we think or meditate on.

Verse 9 of Philippians 4 tells us to stay focus on "those things, which ye have both learned, and received, and heard, and seen in me, do: and the God of peace shall be with you." This verse tells us that we have to learn, receive, and hear, and we have to become doers of the Word of God. Doing what the Word says first builds a mindset of repetitious practice, and this becomes a behavior that forms and develops your life.

This practice also strengthens your belief and builds your faith in the Word of God.

> But whoso looketh into the perfect law of liberty, (the Word of God) and continueth therein, he being not a forgetful hearer, but a doer of the work, this man shall be blessed in his deed. (James 1:25)

We have to become doers of the Word of God.

Hold Fast the Profession (Confession) of Faith

We must continuously speak and confess the Word of God.

> For verily I say unto you, That whosoever shall say unto this mountain, Be thou removed, and be thou cast into the sea; and shall not doubt in his heart, but shall believe that those things which he saith shall come to pass; he shall have whatsoever he saith. (Mark 11:23)

Jesus is saying that we need to speak to our mountains. A mountain is a metaphor for anything that is standing in our way or trying to block our progress. We have to learn to speak to every situation, every opposition, and every hindrance in life. We have to learn to use the Word of God and say what the Word says about the situation and about us.

79

If sickness becomes a mountain, we have to say to this mountain, "Jesus Himself took my infirmities and bore all my sickness and diseases" (Matthew 8:17).

> He was wounded for our transgressions, he was bruised for our iniquities: The chastisement of our peace was upon Him; and with His stripes we are Healed" (Isaiah 53:5).

We have to learn to speak to our financial mountains.

> For ye know the grace of our Lord Jesus Christ, that, though He was rich, yet for my sake He became poor, that I through His poverty might be rich. (2 Corinthians 8:9)

> I wish above all things that thou mayest prosper and be in health, even as thy soul prospereth. (3 John 2)

> But my God shall supply all your need according to his riches in glory by Christ Jesus. (Philippians 4:19)

> Let us hold fast the profession of our faith without wavering; (for he is faithful that promised. (Hebrews 10:23)

Whatever our confession of faith is, we need to hold fast (keep saying it) without wavering (going back and forth with our negative confessions and unbelief). God is faithful. God will do just what He say He will do, we have to do what His Word says, and keep saying what the Word says, and this is holding fast our confession of faith without wavering.

Trusting God

The last part of Isaiah 26:3 states, "Because he trusteth in thee." The *American Heritage Dictionary* defines trust as "to have or place reliance; to depend or place confidence in something or someone, firm reliance on the integrity, ability, or character of a person or thing."

Although trust is a spiritual value, it is not a spiritual characteristic of the fruit of the Holy Spirit. Trust can never replace faith, even though it is very similar. Trust at its best is an emotional, heartfelt gesture that is largely based upon what you know or feel about a person or a thing.

Trust is important because in the absence of trust, fear is implicated.

> There is no fear in love, but perfect love casteth out fear:
> because fear hath torment. He that feareth is not made
> perfect in love (1 John 4:18)

If you have love for someone or something, you should trust—and not have fear—concerning them or it. Without love and trust, fear is implicated.

"Fear hath torment" suggests that it is hard for me trust you because I fear you. Some people are tormented with fear for the lack of trust. It is hard for God to "keep them in perfect peace" for their lack of trust in Him.

Life operates on the principles of trust. We trust doctors with our medical needs, we trust lawyers with our legal needs, and we trust dentist, teachers, and banks with our financial and other needs. However, when it comes to our spiritual needs, trust is sometimes lacking.

It would be almost impossible to embrace life as we know it without trust. *The American Heritage Dictionary* states that trust is built up mainly from the integrity, ability, or character of a person or thing. This lets us know that there has to be some kind of evidence in order to build trust.

Faith versus Trust

Faith is believing without seeing any evidence (Hebrews 11:1). You can have faith in God but not really trust Him, but it is impossible to truly trust God and not have faith in Him. Many of us, after receiving salvation by faith, fail to trust God in some situation. We still have faith, though weak, but we were still saved. Faith was still present, but at that point, we just failed to trust Him. When we trust Him with the salvation of our souls, we have faith in Him. However, there are times when we fail to trust God because of the fear of the unknown.

Trust isn't easy, especially when you've been hurt, knocked down; or wronged by someone or something. Trust is getting back up and taking another chance. Trust is a process, and it doesn't happen overnight. We need to learn to listen to the Holy Spirit in whom and what to trust—and not our own judgments. We need, little by little, to allow people and situations to prove themselves in our lives because the devil can change a person even after you trust them. Jesus trusted Judas with the money and his discipleship, but both the money and his discipleship somehow changed and disappeared.

Ultimately, it is what you know about something or someone that builds trust. The things you learn about them while spending time with them, becoming comfortable in their presence, and trusting their judgments and opinions builds trust.

The Word of the Lord states what the Lord will do if we trust Him. "Thou will keep him in perfect peace" (Isaiah 26:3). Can we trust Him? Can He trust us to trust Him? David said, "Blessed is the man that trust in the Lord" (Psalm 34:18). He is saying you are blessed when you trust the Lord. God does not make mistakes when we put our trust in Him. God might do things His own way, but it is always for our good. He never make mistakes. David learned to trust the Lord.

Solomon said that we should "trust in the Lord with all thine heart, lean not to thine own understanding. In all thy ways acknowledge Him and He shall direct thy path" (Proverbs 3:5). Direction comes from the Lord when we trust Him in all things and lean not to our own judgment. He promised to lead us in the right direction. Solomon learned to trust the Lord.

Job was sick for a long time, and had come down to just existing in sackcloth and ashes. Job said, "Though He slay me, yet will I trust Him" (Job 13:15). Even if God allows us to be slain in our present condition, Job is implying that trust goes beyond death. How can you trust someone after they kill you? Job is saying that he will still trust God even after his death. Job is saying, "God will bring me back or allow me to go on to a better place, and I will trust Him with that decision."

It is important to trust the very source we rely and depend upon to build our confidence because everything we see in this world seems to be negative. There is negativity concerning the economy, the news on television, people in society, and even in the church. They all seem to carry some negativity. We have to learn to trust the Lord through the Word of God. Even though we have been hurt and forsaken, He promised that He "will never leave us nor forsake us."

We can trust Him to "supply all your needs, according to His riches in glory." We can trust Him that when the enemy comes in one way, He will cause him to "flee seven ways." We can trust Him to hold us in the palm of His hands so no one can pluck us out.

We have to learn to trust God and take Him at his Word. One of our greatest challenges is trusting God when things look bad or feel bad. It's hard to trust God when sickness arises or when bills are due, but God promised to keep us in "perfect peace" if we keep our minds stayed on Him and not our problems.

> For our light affliction, which is but for moment, worketh
> for us a far more exceeding and eternal weight of glory,
> while we look not at the things which are seen.
> (2 Corinthians 4:17–18)

We, as believers, have to stop looking at the things that are seen and the problems that present themselves. Looking at problems can diminish our trust and promote fear.

That verse goes on to say that "the things that are seen are temporal." Temporal means it's just a temporary setback, holdup, or distraction. It won't last because it's temporary. The latter part of the verse says that "the things that are not seen are eternal," which is the Word of God. That is what we must continuously look at and trust.

"The Lord is not slack concerning His Promise" (2 Peter 3:9). He will do what He promised to do if we trust Him.

Chapter 11

Eternal Tranquility?
(Peace, Quiet, Rest)

There remaineth therefore a rest to the people of God.
—Hebrews 4:9

The Greek word for tranquility or peace is *eirene,* which means "tranquility rising from without" or "an environmental peace." According to the Word of God, there will not be permanent peace on earth, and there will not be a sustaining peace in the world. Heaven is the only place where there will be a permanent peaceful environment.

There are two kinds of peace: "peace rising from within," which is inner peace (hesuchios), and "peace rising from without," which is outer peace (eirene). The peace rising from without is an environmental peace, as in heaven.

This Greek word for peace, eirene, has a double meaning. The first is peace rising from without, and this next meaning, according to the *World Book Dictionary* is "a harmonious relationship between two (man and God) accomplished through the Gospel; the sense of rest and contentment." Heaven is the place where there will be environmental peace and a "harmonious relationship between God and man, with rest and contentment."

Abraham and Sarah were "looking for a city which hath foundations, whose builder and maker was God" (Hebrews 11:10).

> But now they desire a better country, that is, an heavenly:
> wherefore God is not ashamed to be called their God: for
> He hath prepared for them a city. (Hebrews 11:16)

Heaven is called "a better country" because there is environmental peace there. There is also a "harmonious relationship" between God and man (eirene). Heaven is the final transition we make. This transition is to a place of eternal peace: "eirene" or "peace rising from without." This is the city that Abraham and Sarah were looking for.

> Let not your heart be troubled; ye believe in God, believe
> also in me. In my Father's house are many mansions: if it
> were not so, I would have told you. I go to prepare a place
> for you. (John 14:1–2)

Heaven is an eternal resting place prepared for the born again believer. Jesus said, "And if I go and prepare a place for you, I will come again, and receive you unto myself; that where I am, there ye may be also" (John 14:3). When we are born again, we no longer have permanent residency on earth. We are just temporary citizens. Our permanent residency is in heaven, and our citizenship is permanent there also.

> And I, John, saw the holy city, new Jerusalem, coming
> down from God out of heaven, prepared as a bride adorned
> for her husband. (Revelation 21:2–4)

> And I heard a great voice out of heaven saying, Behold,
> the tabernacle of God is with men, and he will dwell with
> them, and they shall be his people, and God himself shall
> be with them, and be their God. (Revelation 21:3)

There will already be people living in the city of heaven when it arrives:

> And God shall wipe away all tears from their eyes; and
> there shall be no more death, neither sorrow, nor crying,
> neither shall there be any more pain: for the former things
> are passed away. (Revelation 21:4)

These verses explain the eternal peace that we transition to. There will be no more tears or crying. There will be no more death nor sorrow. There will be no more pain or sickness. "The former things are passed away" means we no longer have to be concerned about the things we face here on this earth and in this world. This eternal environment is "peace from without" (eirene).

Chapter 12

Final: Transformation, Transition and Tranquility

We shall not all sleep, but we shall all be changed.
— 1 Corinthians 15:51

This final chapter is a culmination of all three topics: transformation, transition, and tranquility. This scripture in 1 Corinthians 15:51–58 covers all three topics—and what a glorious way to close out this book by including all three topics.

"We shall not all sleep, but we shall all be changed" (1 Corinthians 15:51). The word *transformation* in Greek, according to *Vine's Complete Expository Dictionary*, is *metamorphoo*. According to Google, the English word *metamorphosis* is "the process of transformation from an immature form to an adult form in two or more distinct stages. It's a change of the form or nature of a thing or person into a completely different one by natural or supernatural means."

The Greek word *metamorphoo* means "to change into another form, and to undergo a complete change." Verse 51 states that "we shall all be changed." Verse 52 says, "In a moment, in the twinkling of an eye, at the last trump: for the trumpet shall sound, and the dead shall be raised incorruptible, and we shall be changed." This change that Paul is talking about is from a physical change to a glorified change like unto Jesus's body.

Caught Up Together

For this we say unto you by the word of the Lord, that
we which are alive and remain unto the coming of the
Lord shall not prevent them which are asleep.
—1 Thessalonians 4:15

This verse coincides with 1 Corinthians 15:51, which states that the mystery is that we shall not all sleep, but we shall all be changed.

Paul is explaining there will be some who will be sleeping (dead) and some who will be alive (1 Thessalonians 4:15). But whether asleep or alive, the main thing is that "we shall all be changed."

> In a moment, in the twinkling of an eye, at the last trump:
> for the trumpet shall sound, and the dead shall be raised
> incorruptible, and we shall be changed.
> (1 Corinthians 15:52)

This change here in these verses is called *transformation*.

> For this corruptible must put on incorruption, and this
> mortal must put on immortality. So when this corruptible
> shall have put on incorruption, and this mortal shall have
> put on immortality, then shall be brought to pass the
> saying that is written, Death is swallowed up in victory.
> (1 Corinthians 15:53–54)

Since "flesh and blood cannot inherit the kingdom" (1 Corinthians 15:50), the body must undergo a glorified change. These verses states that the flesh or body is *corrupt* and *corruptible*. For this reason, the flesh cannot inherit the kingdom of God. A glorified change is simply putting off this fleshly body and putting on a spiritual body as unto Jesus.

> Beloved, now are we the sons of God, and it doth not yet
> appear what we shall be: but we know that, when he shall
> appear, we shall be like Him; for we shall see him as he
> is. (1 John 3:2)

When we see Jesus, we will be transformed and be like unto His own glorious body. We shall be like Him. This glorified body, which is like unto Jesus's own glorious body, is not subject to sickness, death, or pain:

> And God shall wipe away all tears from their eyes; and
> there shall be no more death, neither sorrow, nor crying,

neither shall there be any more pain: for the former things
are passed away. (Revelation 21:4)

In this glorified state, there is no death and no pain. There will be no
need to cry or weep because we will not be subject to hurt or pain.

The final transition that will take place is 1 Thessalonians 4:17:

Then we which are alive and remain shall be caught up
together with them in the clouds, to meet the Lord in the
air: and so shall we ever be with the Lord.

The Greek word for "caught up" or "raised up" is *exergeiro*, which
means "to be raised" "out of or into a place, or position."

Some people will be alive, and some people will be dead, but those
of us who are alive and remain shall be caught up together with the dead
in Jesus Christ in the clouds. We will not just meet Him; we will be with
Him forever (1 Thessalonians 4:17). What a time this will be as we enjoy
the final transition to eternal peace and tranquility.

References

Word of Faith Magazine (2015). Kenneth Hagin Ministries. Tulsa, OK.

Metamorphosis (2016). Retrieved May 16, 2016, from Google.com.

Vine, W. E., Unger, Merrill F., and White Jr., William. (1996). *Vine's Complete Expository Dictionary of Old and New Testament Words.* Thomas Nelson Publishers: Nashville, Atlanta, London, Vancouver.

The World Book Dictionary. (1991). William H. Nault, Publisher; World Book, Inc.

The King James Open Bible. 1990. Thomas Nelson, Inc.

The World Book Encyclopedia. 1991. World Book, Inc.

Why? Because You Are Anointed, (1994). T.D. Jakcs; Destiny Image, Publishers, Inc.; Shippensburg, PA.

The Purpose Driven Life. (2002). Rick Warren; Zondervan, Grand Rapids, MI.

The New Strong's Compact Bible Concordance, 2004. Thomas Nelson Publishers. Nashville, TN.

The American Heritage Dictionary. (October 16, 2018). Houghton Mifflin Harcourt; Indexed Edition.

The New Open Bible Study Edition. 1990. Thomas Nelson Publisher, Nashville, TN.

Horne, Thomas. (2013). *Are You the One?* iUniverse, Bloomington, IN.

Evans, Tony. (2005). *Let It Go.* Moody Publishers, Chicago, IL.

Merriam Webster Collegiate Dictionary 11th Edition. (2003). Springfield, Mass.

Horne, Thomas. (2009). *The Truth about Faith*, Quality Instant Printing Pub., Durham, NC.

Wesley, John, April 25, 2019. Google: "I set myself on fire and people come to watch me burn."

Printed in the United States
by Baker & Taylor Publisher Services

Printed in the United States
by Baker & Taylor Publisher Services